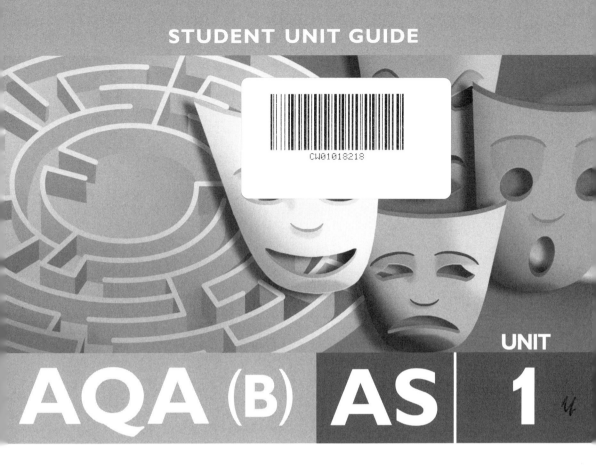

CW01018218

AQA (B) | AS | UNIT 1

Psychology

Introducing Psychology

Julie McLoughlin

Philip Allan Updates, an imprint of Hodder Education, an Hachette UK company, Market Place, Deddington, Oxfordshire OX15 0SE

Orders

Bookpoint Ltd, 130 Milton Park, Abingdon, Oxfordshire OX14 4SB
tel: 01235 827720
fax: 01235 400454
e-mail: uk.orders@bookpoint.co.uk
Lines are open 9.00 a.m.–5.00 p.m., Monday to Saturday, with a 24-hour message answering service. You can also order through the Philip Allan Updates website: www.philipallan.co.uk

© Philip Allan Updates 2008

ISBN 978-0-340-95953-4

First printed 2008
Impression number 5 4 3
Year 2013 2012 2011 2010

This guide has been written specifically to support students preparing for the AQA Specification B AS Psychology Unit 1 examination. The content has been neither approved nor endorsed by AQA and remains the sole responsibility of the author.

Typeset by Pantek Arts Ltd, Maidstone
Printed by MPG Books, Bodmin

Hachette Livre UK's policy is to use papers that are natural, renewable and recyclable products and made from wood grown in sustainable forests. The logging and manufacturing processes are expected to conform to the environmental regulations of the country of origin.

Contents

Introduction

■ ■ ■

Content Guidance

■ ■ ■

Questions and Answers

Introduction

About this guide

This is a guide to Unit 1 of the AQA(B) AS psychology specification. The guide is intended as a revision *aid* rather than as a textbook. The purpose of the guide is to summarise the content, to explain how the content will be assessed, to look at the type of questions to expect, and to consider specimen answers.

The whole of Unit 1 is compulsory, which means that you must cover everything to be able to answer any questions that appear on the examination paper. In this unit there is no choice of questions. Topic areas covered in the guide are Key Approaches in Psychology and Biopsychology, Gender Development and Research Methods. For each of the topic areas on the specification this guide covers the following:

- the specification content, including exactly what you need to know and learn. The coverage of the content is minimal as you should already have covered the details in your studies. The focus is on key terms and concepts, key theories and studies, and evaluation points. The content here is not the only appropriate material; textbooks will cover the topics in various ways and probably give much more detail and alternative studies.
- two example questions from each of the main topic areas, making a total of six questions. These questions are in the style of AQA(B) questions and similar to those that you might expect to see on real examination papers. To accompany each question there is an analysis of how the question should be tackled and what the examiners are looking for in an answer.
- for each question there are *two* sample answers, A and B. One answer is typical of a borderline grade C/D performance and the other is a high-scoring answer typical of those awarded a grade A. Each answer is followed by a detailed commentary about the marks that have been awarded, drawing attention to any errors or points that are especially creditworthy. There are also suggestions as to how the answers might be improved or elaborated to get extra marks. If you read these sample answers and comments carefully you will learn a lot about what you need to do to present an effective answer in the examination.

How to use this guide

First check your class notes and revision notes against the content presented here to make sure that you have all the *right* material for your revision. Then look at a sample question to see how the examination is structured and what is required. Have a go at the question yourself; then review the sample answers and comments to see where credit can be gained and lost. The sample answers are not intended as model answers but as tools to help you understand what makes a good answer. Finally, you should review your own answer in the light of what you have read and consider how your own response to the question might be improved.

The examination

The Unit 1 examination is $1\frac{1}{2}$ hours long and you have to answer three questions: one on Approaches (including Biopsychology), one on Gender Development and one on Research Methods. Each question carries *20 marks* so you should allow 30 minutes for each question in the examination.

The Approaches and Gender Development questions are structured, which means that there are several sub-sections to each question. The first sub-sections are usually short-answer questions worth *1*, *2*, *3* or *4 marks*. These are followed by a final sub-section that requires extended writing for *10 marks*.

Short-answer questions

- Commands like 'Identify', 'State', 'Name', 'Suggest' and 'Give' require the briefest answers.
- Commands like 'Outline' and 'Describe' require straightforward description.
- Commands like 'Explain' and 'Distinguish' require some analysis or elaboration of concepts. In the case of 'Distinguish', you need to explain the difference(s) between two points.
- The command 'Briefly discuss' requires some description and some evaluation or criticism and is usually worth *4* or *5 marks*.
- If asked to 'Describe a study' for *4 marks*, you should refer explicitly to the aim, method, results and conclusion.

Examples of short-answer questions

'Identify **two** assumptions of the humanistic approach.'

'Explain what is meant by *free will*.'

'Give an example of modelling.'

'State what is meant by *qualitative research*.'

'Outline what psychologists mean by the term *androgyny*.'

'Describe **one** study in which classical conditioning was investigated.'

'Briefly discuss **one** limitation of the case study method.'

'Distinguish between imitation and identification.'

Long-answer questions

These are worth *10 marks*. A typical 10-mark question would ask you to 'Describe and evaluate' a theory, an explanation or some research. In 10-mark questions, *5 marks* are for description and *5 marks* are for evaluation/analysis/application. In the evaluation, you should present strengths and limitations. If relevant, you should support what you say with reference to evidence and explain how the evidence relates to the topic. You can also get evaluation marks by comparing — for example, introducing an opposing theory to illustrate the limitations of the theory you are discussing. You should aim to spend plenty of time on this sub-section of the question in the examination.

In the 10-mark questions you will be assessed on your ability to communicate. You should therefore make sure that your answer is properly structured into sentences and paragraphs, and pay attention to your spelling. If a 10-mark question asks you to 'refer to evidence' or 'refer to an alternative explanation', there will be a limit to the number of marks that you will be awarded if you do not comply with that instruction.

Mark schemes for 10-mark questions are banded into 'good', 'average' and 'poor' bands. This means that the examiner will not only consider each individual point that you make, but will also make a global assessment of the answer as a whole. Candidates who show lots of knowledge and make many evaluation points but do not present a well-argued response will generally be awarded a lower mark than they might have been given. This is because the answer as a whole is better suited to the 'average' band rather than the 'good' band.

Scenario questions

In some questions you must use your knowledge by applying what you have learned about psychology to a novel situation. For example, a question might include a scenario about someone who is on a scary roller-coaster ride. In this case, you might be required to use your knowledge of the autonomic nervous system to explain the physiological reactions of the person in the scenario. For example, you could describe how the person's heart-rate would increase and their digestion would slow down. This sort of question tests the application of knowledge.

Research Methods questions

Unit 1 has one full question on Research Methods. This is more heavily structured than the other questions, consisting of several sub-sections requiring short answers. There is no 10-mark sub-section in the Research Methods question. In addition to the full question on Research Methods, there may be sub-sections assessing knowledge and understanding of Research Methods and practical psychology in other questions. For example, there may be a Gender Development question in which you are asked how gender stereotyping has been studied by psychologists.

Assessment objectives

Examination boards use the term 'assessment objective' (AO) to refer to the different types of skills that you are expected to demonstrate in examinations. Your teacher might have told you about AO1, AO2 and AO3 skills.

- AO1 refers to knowledge and understanding.
- AO2 refers to analysis and evaluation and the application of knowledge to novel situations.
- AO3 refers to knowledge and understanding of Research Methods and practical psychology.

You should not worry too much about these different skills in the examination. In most cases the wording of the question will lead you to demonstrate the necessary skills. Only the following two types of question require you to think about AO skills:

- In 10-mark questions, *5 marks* are for description (AO1) and *5 marks* are for evaluation, analysis and application (AO2). In a 10-mark question, you should aim to present a balance of description and evaluation/analysis/application. These will usually ask you to 'Describe and evaluate' or 'Discuss'.
- 'Briefly discuss' for *3, 4* or *5 marks* — here there would normally be *1* or *2 marks* for description (AO1) and 2 or *3 marks* for evaluation, analysis and application (AO2).

Content Guidance

The topics covered in the Content Guidance section are:

- **Approaches**
  - Key approaches in psychology
  - Biopsychology: physiological psychology
  - Biopsychology: genetic basis of behaviour
- **Gender development**
  - Concepts
  - Explaining gender development
- **Research methods**
  - Planning research
  - Experimental methods
  - Non-experimental methods
  - Representing data and descriptive statistics
  - Ethics

Approaches
Key approaches in psychology

Specification content

The basic assumptions of the following approaches: biological; behaviourist; social learning theory; cognitive; psychodynamic; and humanistic. The distinguishing features of each approach, including research methods used. The strengths and limitations of each approach.

Biological approach

The biological approach focuses on ways in which our biological make-up influences our thoughts and behaviour. In recent years, with the development of more sophisticated scientific techniques and laboratory procedures, the biological approach has become increasingly important in psychology.

The **basic assumptions/features** of the biological approach are as follows:
- **Genes** influence behaviour.
- **Biological structures**, such as the brain and nervous system, influence behaviour.
- **Brain chemistry** influences behaviour.
- Behaviour has **evolved**: behaviours that help us survive are more likely to be passed on to future generations than behaviours that do not help us survive.
- There is **behavioural continuity** between species, so it makes sense to study animal species and make a generalisation to human behaviour.

Research methods
Methods typically used by biological psychologists include surgery (e.g. experiments using animals to see the effects of lesions to the hippocampus on memory); the use of brain-recording techniques and scans, like MRI and PET scans, to observe the activity of living brains in human participants; experiments to test the effects of drugs (e.g. the effects of medication on children with autism); analysis of case studies of individuals who have suffered some kind of brain damage to see how their behaviour has been affected; twin studies to see how alike identical and non-identical twins are for various characteristics.

Strengths of the biological approach

- The methods are highly scientific.
- Knowing how biology is involved in psychological disorders enables researchers to find suitable treatments.

Limitations of the biological approach

- At its most extreme, it neglects the possible influences of social factors and environment.
- Explaining complex behaviours at the levels of cells and chemicals is an oversimplification. This is known as reductionism.

- It seems to suggest that the mind and the brain are the same thing.
- It suggests that people do not have free will to decide how to behave. This is known as biological determinism.
- There are ethical implications. For example, if behaviour such as criminality is found to be genetic, what should we do about it?
- There are problems generalising findings from animal research to humans.

Behaviourist approach

Behaviourism developed in the USA in the early twentieth century and was for a long time the dominant approach in psychology. Behaviourists carried out highly controlled experiments to investigate how behaviour is learned. The **basic assumptions/features** of the behaviourist approach are as follows:

- All behaviour is **learned** and can be understood in terms of stimulus–response (SR) links.
- Behaviour depends on **consequences**. If a behaviour has a pleasant consequence then it is likely to be repeated. If it has an unpleasant consequence then it is not likely to be repeated.
- Psychology should be **scientific** and **objective**. Psychologists should only study observable behaviour; mental processes like memory and attention are not appropriate subject matter for psychologists.
- It is sensible to generalise from animal research to human behaviour.

Research methods

Behaviourist psychologists normally conduct controlled laboratory experiments, often using animals as subjects.

Classical conditioning

Classical conditioning theory was used by the behaviourists to explain simple learned associations. Pavlov studied salivation in dogs. He found that by pairing food with the sound of a bell, a dog learned to associate the food and bell. After a number of pairings, the bell alone would produce salivation in the dog. The dog had been conditioned to respond to a previously neutral stimulus. Pavlov termed this process 'classical conditioning' and it is shown in the table below, which charts the progression from unconditioned stimulus to conditioned response. Classical conditioning is a basic form of learning that can only be applied to involuntary reflex behaviours such as salivation, eye blinking and fear.

Stages involved in classical conditioning

Stage 1	Food (UCS)	elicits	salivation (UCR)
Stage 2	Food (UCS) + bell (CS)	elicits	salivation (UCR)
Stage 3	Bell (CS)	elicits	salivation (CR)

UCS = unconditioned stimulus; CS = conditioned stimulus; UCR = unconditioned response; CR = conditioned response

Classical conditioning was demonstrated in humans by Watson and Raynor (1920), who conditioned a fear of white furry things in a baby, Little Albert, by repeatedly making a loud noise every time he played with his pet white rat.

The following key concepts are associated with classical conditioning:
- **generalisation** — producing the conditioned response to a stimulus that is similar to the original conditioned stimulus
- **discrimination** — not responding to a stimulus that is different from the original conditioned stimulus
- **extinction** — a conditioned response dies out after repeated presentation of the conditioned stimulus without the unconditioned stimulus

Operant conditioning

Operant conditioning theory was used by the behaviourists to explain how voluntary behaviours are learned. Skinner (1953) carried out experiments with rats using a Skinner Box. He found that rats would quickly learn to associate pressing a bar with food. Skinner described the food as **reinforcement** since it strengthened the learned behaviour, making it more likely to occur. The different types of reinforcement are as follows:
- **positive reinforcement** — a pleasant stimulus is received after a behaviour is performed
- **negative reinforcement** — a behaviour is performed to avoid an unpleasant stimulus (avoidance learning)
- **punishment**: an unpleasant stimulus is received after a behaviour is performed
- **primary reinforcement** — something that is in itself rewarding, e.g. sweets
- **secondary reinforcement** — something that is not in itself rewarding but can be exchanged for something that is, e.g. tokens, money

Strengths of the behaviourist approach

- It uses highly controlled scientific methods.
- It enables the prediction of behaviour.
- Many therapies have been derived from behaviourist theory, e.g. token economy systems where people in institutions are given tokens for good behaviour. These tokens can later be exchanged for treats.

Limitations of the behaviourist approach

- It assumes that biological factors have little influence on behaviour.
- It neglects mental processes and emotions.
- Behaviour is seen as being determined by the environment, suggesting there is no free will. This is known as environmental determinism.
- It may not be sensible to generalise from animal research to human behaviour.
- Seeing all behaviour in terms of simple SR links is an oversimplification.

Social learning theory

Social learning theory was developed in the 1960s to take account of the importance of social factors and mental processes in human learning. Social learning theorists focused on observational learning in humans. The **basic assumptions/features** of social learning theory are listed on p. 14:

- Behaviour is learned through **observation** and **imitation**.
- **Modelling** is copying the behaviour of people with whom we identify.
- **Identification** with someone involves a desire to be like them and therefore leads to a desire to imitate them.
- Reinforcement can be **vicarious** — we can learn through observation of the consequences for others of their actions.
- **Mediating cognitive factors** (like memory and thinking) occur between stimulus and response; we do not observe and automatically imitate but think about several factors before we imitate. For example, we would think about whether we are physically able to carry out the action we have observed, and whether we want to or not. We are more likely to produce modelling behaviour if the model is perceived to be attractive, of high status and similar to ourselves. Also, we are more likely to show modelling behaviour if the behaviour is seen to be appropriate and if the model is seen to be rewarded.

Research methods

Social learning theorists usually carry out experiments with human participants, with observational techniques used to gather data. In a sequence of studies, Bandura, Ross and Ross (1960s) showed children an adult (a model) behaving aggressively towards an inflatable Bobo doll. It was found that the children would model the behaviour, although the likelihood of modelling occurring depended on factors such as the characteristics of the model and whether he/she was seen to be rewarded or punished.

Strengths of social learning theory

- It considers the role of cognitive factors in learning.
- It explains the learning of complex human behaviours such as aggression.

Limitations of social learning theory

- The Bobo doll experiment is highly artificial. It lacks ecological validity.
- The assumption that all behaviour is learned neglects the role of biology in behaviour.

Cognitive approach

The cognitive approach became popular in the 1950s and 1960s with the development of computers. Cognitive psychologists focus on internal mental processing and the influence of thought on behaviour. The **basic assumptions/features** of the cognitive approach are as follows:
- **Internal mental processes**, like memory and perception, can be studied scientifically.
- Humans **actively** process information.
- Human information processing is similar to the way a **computer** processes information, proceeding through a sequence of stages from **input** to **output**.
- Theoretical **models** (structured theories usually represented as flow charts) can be used to explain cognitive processes.

One model used to explain cognitive processes is the multi-store model of memory (Atkinson and Shiffrin 1968). The model presents memory as a stage-based sequence in the form of a flow chart. This is typical of how cognitive psychologists use models to explain cognitive processes.

Research methods

Methods typically used by cognitive psychologists include controlled laboratory experiments investigating mental processes in human participants; case studies of single individuals who have a cognitive impairment (e.g. a memory disorder or language problem); computer modelling of human processes (e.g a computer face-recognition programme); use of scans to enable investigation of the neurological activity when various cognitive processes are taking place.

A typical study of internal mental processing is a memory experiment where participants hear a list of unconnected words and then have to recall them in any order. It is usually found that participants recall the first and last words on the list, but tend to recall few from the middle. This is known as the primacy–recency effect. These findings have been used to understand the way that memory works; it is suggested that the first words on the list have been rehearsed and therefore are recalled from long-term memory, whereas the last words on the list are recalled from short-term memory.

Strengths of the cognitive approach

- It considers the role of thinking in behaviour.
- Cognitive models help to explain complex thinking processes by separating a complex process into its separate components.
- It focuses on investigations using human participants.
- It uses highly controlled scientific methods.
- Successful therapies have been developed using cognitive principles, e.g. cognitive behaviour therapy for depression, where the therapist tries to get the depressed person to have more positive thoughts.

Limitations of the cognitive approach

- Traditional cognitive research relies on inference; we can only guess about what mental processes are taking place on the basis of the results of an experiment.
- The cognitive approach says little about the initial causes of behaviour.
- It takes a mechanistic view, likening human processing to the workings of a machine.
- Cognitive experiments tend to be highly artificial, lacking in ecological validity.

Psychodynamic approach

The psychodynamic approach was initiated by Freud at the beginning of the twentieth century. Freud emphasised the **role of the unconscious**, suggesting that we are consciously aware of only a small proportion of our thought, and that our unconscious wishes and fears influence our conscious behaviour and our personality. The **basic assumptions/features** of the psychodynamic approach are as follows:

- **Unconscious** mental processes motivate our behaviour.
- Personality has three parts: the **id**, which is unreasonably demanding and self-serving, like a little child who demands instant satisfaction; the **superego**, which is the over-demanding, strict and punishing internal parent or conscience that makes us feel guilty; the **ego**, which is the conscious self resulting from the competing demands of the id and the superego.

- **Early childhood experiences** influence adult behaviour and personality. Problems like anxiety in adult life are often due to unpleasant early experiences of which we are not consciously aware.
- Development takes place in **psychosexual stages**. At each stage the child derives satisfaction from a different area of the body, for example, in the oral stage the child enjoys oral stimulation from breast or bottle feeding. At each stage there is a conflict to be resolved; if this conflict is not satisfactorily resolved, then the child will become fixated at that stage. As an example, the conflict in the oral stage revolves around weaning. If there are problems at the weaning stage then the person will have an oral fixation, engaging in oral behaviours such as nail-biting in adulthood.
- **Defence mechanisms** are unconscious processes that act to protect the conscious self from unpleasant events in the world or unpleasant thoughts about the self. Examples include: denial — refusing to believe that an unpleasant event is happening; repression — motivated forgetting.
- Psychological problems can be treated through accessing the unconscious using methods involved in the Freudian therapy known as **psychoanalysis**, such as free association or analysis of dreams.

Research methods

The main method used in the psychodynamic approach is the case study. This is because most research in this area has been carried out with individual cases of people who consulted Freud and other psychoanalysts because they were suffering from neurotic or anxiety disorders. One such case is Little Hans, a young boy who was suffering from a phobia of horses. Freud suggested that Little Hans was not really afraid of horses but in fact was afraid of his father (see p. 34).

Strengths of the psychodynamic approach

- Freud recognised the importance of childhood experiences for later life.
- The idea of unconscious mental activity is appealing.
- Defence mechanisms offer plausible explanations for everyday behaviour and experiences.
- Psychoanalysis has had some reported success and has led to the development of other psychological therapies.

Limitations of the psychodynamic approach

- It is often accused of being male-oriented.
- It over-emphasises the sexual instinct as a motivating factor, even suggesting that it influences childhood behaviour.
- The theories and concepts are not based on scientific evidence.
- The unconscious cannot be verified or tested. As such, the theory is unfalsifiable.
- Freud is often accused of fitting his cases to his already existing theory.
- It is inappropriate to base a theory of all human behaviour on just a few case studies.
- It focuses on the past, stressing the negative effects of past experiences.

Humanistic approach

The humanistic approach became popular in the 1960s as part of a rejection of the mechanistic science of the behaviourists and the pessimism of psychoanalysis. Humanistic psychologists rejected the scientific approach in psychology because they believed that the focus should be on the individual and therefore it is not sensible to make generalisations. The approach is sometimes described as being 'anti-science'. The **basic assumptions/features** of the humanistic approach are as follows:

- People have the **free will** to determine their own destiny. This is in contrast to the determinism of the biological and behaviourist approaches.
- The emphasis is on the **self**. Carl Rogers felt that psychological problems were due to differences between the perceived self and the ideal self. He referred to this difference as incongruence. Rogers suggested that incongruence between the perceived and ideal self are due to other people, usually parents, imposing **conditions of worth**. In other words, loving and accepting their children only if they fulfil certain conditions. To counter this, Rogers suggested that people need unconditional positive regard — to be loved and accepted for what they are.
- All people have a unique experience of the world (their own **phenomenology**).
- Everyone is essentially good and in the right conditions can grow and **self-actualise** (reach their full potential).
- Behaviour is motivated by a **hierarchy of needs** with basic survival needs at the bottom and the need to self-actualise (be fulfilled) at the top.
- Therapy should be **client-centred**. It should also be **holistic** (considering all aspects of a person), **empathic** (appreciating the client's feelings) and genuine.

Research methods

Humanistic psychologists study individuals using the case study method or study people interacting in group therapy sessions. One of the few attempts at objective measurement is a test known as the Q-sort, where people have to sort cards into piles according to whether they think the description on the card is like them or not. The Q-sort is used to test a person's self-perception.

Strengths of the humanistic approach

- It offers a more optimistic and forward-looking view of human nature than the psychodynamic approach.
- It credits the person as being responsible for their own behaviour.
- Client-centred therapy is effective for minor problems and has led to the growth of counselling.

Limitations of the humanistic approach

- Perhaps it is unrealistically optimistic; maybe some people can never self-actualise.
- The concepts of self and self-actualisation may not apply in other cultures, for example, collectivist cultures such as China.
- It is unscientific, rejecting scientific methods and principles. This means that humanistic ideas and concepts cannot be properly investigated.
- The focus on the individual means that generalisations cannot be made about all human behaviour.

Biopsychology: physiological psychology

Specification content

Neurons and synaptic transmission. The divisions of the nervous system. Localisation of function in the brain. Methods used to identify areas of cortical specialisation. Actions of the sympathetic and parasympathetic divisions of the autonomic nervous system.

Neurons and synaptic transmission

Neurons are nerve cells. The human nervous system has around 100 billion neurons. Neurons send and receive electrical information, or nerve impulses, either from other neurons, or other cells (e.g. muscle cells, heart cells).

- **Sensory neurons** carry information from the senses to the central nervous system.
- **Motor neurons** transmit messages from the central nervous system to the muscles.
- **Interneurons** (connector neurons) connect neurons to other neurons. Approximately 95% of these are in the brain.

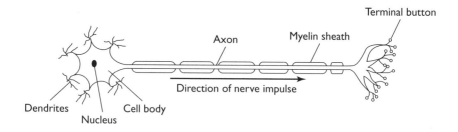

Figure 1 A motor neuron

A neuron (see Figure 1) has a **cell body**, an **axon** and branch-like **dendrites**. The cell body has a nucleus containing our **DNA** or genetic material. Within the cell, information travels by means of electrical impulses. The axon extends from the cell body. Axons are covered with a fatty **myelin sheath**, which insulates the axon and speeds up transmission of electrical impulses along it. The **terminal button** at the end of the axon houses **vesicles** (tiny sacs) containing chemicals known as **neurotransmitters**. Adjacent neurons do not actually touch one another, between them is a gap known as the **synapse** or synaptic cleft. When an electrical impulse travels to the end of the axon, the vesicles release their neurotransmitter across the synapse. This chemical then locks into special receptor sites on the dendrite of the adjacent neuron. From there the electrical nerve impulse is transmitted in the same way through the next neuron. Some neurotransmitters increase the rate of firing between neurons whilst others decrease the rate of firing. The movement of an electrical impulse along the axon is called an **action potential.** This happens when a chemical process alters the electric charge, both inside and outside of the neuron.

Neurotransmitters

Neurotransmitters are brain chemicals that affect cognitive processes and behaviour.

- **Acetylcholine (ACH)** is found at synapses between motor neurons and muscle cells and is responsible for movement.
- **Dopamine** affects arousal, pleasure and voluntary movement. Too much dopamine is thought to be responsible for schizophrenia.
- **Serotonin** governs sleep, aggression and mood. Low levels of serotonin are associated with depression.

Divisions of the nervous system

The human nervous system is divided into the central nervous system and the peripheral nervous system, as shown in Figure 2.

The **central nervous system** is made up of the brain and spinal cord. The spinal cord receives and passes messages to and from the brain, and connects to nerves in the peripheral nervous system.

The **peripheral nervous system** consists of neurons that send information to and from the central nervous system. It is divided into the somatic and autonomic nervous systems.

The **somatic nervous system** transmits information received by the senses to the central nervous system and sends messages from the central nervous system to the muscles.

The **autonomic nervous system** is divided into the sympathetic and parasympathetic sections. The autonomic nervous system links the central nervous system to internal organs and controls basic functions such as breathing and digestion. It cannot be controlled voluntarily.

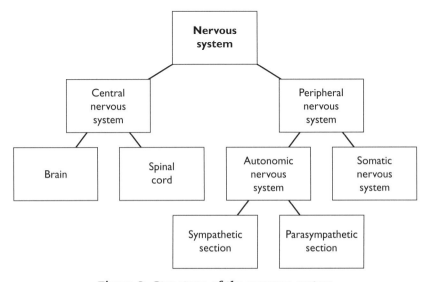

Figure 2 Structure of the nervous system

Localisation of function

The notion that different areas of the brain have different functions is known as localisation of function. The human brain has two hemispheres responsible for higher cognitive functions, such as thinking and remembering. They are joined by the **corpus callosum**, a set of nerve fibres allowing information to be transferred between the two hemispheres. The right hemisphere is mostly responsible for the left side of the body, and the left hemisphere for the right side of the body. Lateralisation of function refers to the way that the two hemispheres have different functions (also referred to as hemispheric specialisation). In right-handed people the left side of the brain is most important for language function, logic and analysis and the right side is most important for non-linguistic processing (e.g. music and emotion). The opposite is true for people who are left-handed.

Different functions are located in different areas of the cortex:
- Movement is located in the motor cortex to the rear of the frontal lobe.
- Sensory processing (touch) is located in the somatosensory cortex in the parietal lobe, to the rear of the motor cortex.
- Vision is located in the visual cortex in the occipital lobe at the rear of the cortex.
- Auditory (sound) processing is located in the left temporal lobe.

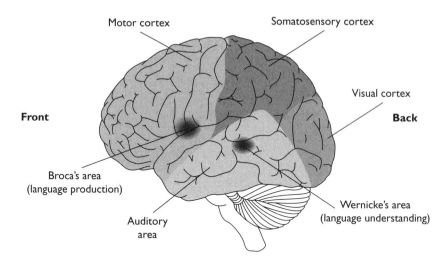

Figure 3 Different areas of the brain

Localisation of language

Broca's area, to the left of the frontal lobe, governs speech production. Damage to Broca's area causes speech to be slow and laborious. **Wernicke's area**, in the left temporal lobe, governs the understanding of speech. Damage to this area causes comprehension problems and the person's speech is fluent but meaningless. Studies using brain scans have shown that either Broca's area or Wernicke's area is active when people perform different types of language task. For example, listening to nouns involves Wernicke's area, and thinking of verbs to go in a phrase uses Broca's area (Peterson et al. 1988).

Evaluation

- Although some functions can be located in certain areas of the brain, most functions involve many inter-connected areas of the brain. In other words, brain function is **holistic**.
- People with brain damage to a specific area (e.g. after a stroke) often recover function over time because another area of the brain takes over. This is referred to as **brain plasticity**.

Methods used to identify cortical specialisation

Neurosurgery

Neurosurgery involves the destruction of an area of the brain. A surgical procedure known as **lobotomy** was formerly used to treat mental disorders. This usually involved severing the frontal lobes, resulting in loss of personality, passivity and lack of emotion. This procedure is rarely used these days, although animal researchers sometimes deliberately use surgical procedures to see how damage to certain areas of the brain affects behaviour. Occasionally there are psychological effects following brain operations carried out to treat conditions such as epilepsy. Such a case is that of HM, whose hippocampus was damaged during an operation. The surgical damage affected his ability to make any new memories.

Post-mortem examinations

A post-mortem examination involves surgical dissection of the brain of a person who has died. Paul Broca (1824–80) used post-mortem examinations in an attempt to link visible signs of brain damage with how the person had behaved when they were alive. This is how he discovered that language function was located on the left side of the brain.

Electroencephalograms (EEGs)

EEGs record the electrical activity of areas of the brain using electrodes that are placed on the head. Brain wave patterns coming from the activity of lots of neurons can be seen on a screen. EEGs have been used to study normal brain activity and brain activity in cases of conditions such as epilepsy. They give an overall picture of brain activity and have become more sophisticated, with computers used to analyse recordings from large numbers of electrodes.

Electrical stimulation

One form of electrical stimulation involves the insertion of an electrode into a single neuron, which is then stimulated with electricity. A second form of electrical stimulation involves an area of the brain rather than just a single neuron. Penfield and Rasmussen (1950) asked people to report their feelings and experiences when parts of the cortex were stimulated. People sometimes reported hearing music. Electrical stimulation of the brain using implanted electrodes has been used to successfully treat chronic pain (Kumar et al. 1990).

Scans

Positron-emission tomography (PET) involves the injection of a radioactive chemical into the bloodstream. The head is then scanned to see the amount of radioactivity coming from different parts of the brain. The amount of radioactivity increases with increased blood flow, indicating which areas of the brain are most active. PET scans can be used to see which parts of the brain are involved in different mental tasks, such as reading. Scanning techniques have greatly advanced understanding of brain function, can be used with live human brains, and are more accurate and less invasive than many other methods. MRI and CAT are other types of scans used to study brain structure and function.

Autonomic nervous system

The autonomic nervous system connects the central nervous system with smooth muscled organs and glands and is part of the **peripheral nervous system**. The functions of the autonomic nervous system (e.g. increased heart rate) are not normally under conscious control. The autonomic nervous system is divided into the sympathetic and parasympathetic sections. The **sympathetic section** prepares the body for action in an emergency or exciting situation. The **parasympathetic section** has the opposite effect, bringing the body back to its normal state. Imagine that you are walking alone down a dark lane at night and you hear a noise. The action of the sympathetic section of the autonomic nervous system prepares you for 'fight or flight'. When the danger has passed, the action of the parasympathetic section restores your body functions back to their normal state.

*Effects of the sympathetic and parasympathetic sections
of the autonomic nervous system*

Sympathetic action	Parasympathetic action
Heart rate increases	Heart rate decreases
Pupil dilates	Pupil constricts
Intestine/gut action slows	Intestine/gut action restored
Salivation stops (mouth dries)	Salivation restored

Endocrine system: the adrenal glands

Glands in the **endocrine system** secrete **hormones** into the bloodstream. These are chemical messengers that affect body organs. The **pituitary gland** is the 'master gland'; the hormones it releases regulate the activity of other glands. The pituitary gland is controlled by the **hypothalamus** in the brain.

Role of the adrenal glands in stress

The adrenal gland is involved in stress in two separate ways:
- The brain stimulates the sympathetic nervous system, which in turn stimulates the adrenal gland to release adrenalin. This causes the 'adrenalin rush' that we experience at times of stress or anxiety (e.g. when tripping on the stairs).

- The hypothalamus stimulates the pituitary gland, which instructs the adrenal gland to release the hormone cortisol. Cortisol activates the release of glucose into the bloodstream for energy.

Glands of the endocrine system and their main functions

Gland	Function
Pituitary gland	Master gland, controls other glands
Thyroid gland	Produces thyroxin, for regulation of growth and metabolism
Adrenal gland	Produces adrenalin, responsible for the fight or flight reaction
Ovaries	Produce oestrogen and progesterone, responsible for female sexual behaviour
Testes	Produce testosterone, responsible for male sexual behaviour

Biopsychology: genetic basis of behaviour

Specification content

The difference between genotype and phenotype. Types of twins and the use of twin studies, family studies and adoption studies to investigate the genetic basis of behaviour.

Genetics is the study of genetic make-up and the influence of our genes on physical characteristics and behaviour. **Genes** are found in the nucleus of every cell and are located on **chromosomes** (bundles of genes) that exist in 23 pairs. This genetic material is passed on from parent to child through sexual reproduction. Biopsychologists believe that psychological traits, such as personality and intelligence, are determined by our genetic make-up in the same way as physical traits.

Genotype and phenotype

A distinction is made between the **genotype**, a person's genetic make-up, and their **phenotype**, the actual expression of the genes in an individual. As an example, it is possible that a person may carry a gene for a certain disease (it is part of their genotype), but they might never actually develop the disease (it is not in their phenotype). Identical twins have the same genotype because they share 100% of their genes. However, they may not share the same phenotype; one of them may be stronger and more muscular than the other because he works out at the gym.

The genotype interacts with environmental influences to produce the phenotype. This can be clearly seen in the genetic condition **phenylketonuria** (PKU). PKU sufferers cannot metabolise phenylalanine, which means that they will have brain damage if they are untreated. However, with a special phenylalanine-free diet, the baby will develop normally. This means that two people with the same PKU genotype could demonstrate quite different phenotypes, one brain damaged and the other quite normal. Such examples show us that genes alone cannot explain psychological traits and behaviour: environmental factors are also important.

Types of twins

- **Monozygotic twins (MZ)** develop from a single fertilised egg. They share 100% of their genes. MZ twins are referred to as identical twins.
- **Dizygotic twins (DZ)** develop from two different eggs that have been fertilised by different sperm. They share 50% of their genes, the same as any two siblings (brothers or sisters). DZ twins are referred to as non-identical or fraternal twins.

Twin studies

Twin studies investigate the degree of similarity (**concordance**) between MZ twin pairs and DZ twin pairs. If a trait is genetic, MZ twins should be more alike for that trait than DZ twins. One problem with twin studies is that MZ twins are often treated more similarly than DZ twins. This means that they may behave more alike simply because they have been treated in the same way, rather than because they share exactly the same genes. To avoid this problem, psychologists try to study identical twins reared apart, although there are few cases.

Study

Bouchard et al. (1990) reported on a longitudinal study of intelligence in twins, both MZ and DZ, some of whom had been reared together and some of whom had been reared apart. All twins born in Minnesota between 1961 and 1964 took part. MZ twins had more similar intelligence test scores than DZ twins. The same effect was found whether the twins had been reared together or apart.

Study

Gottesman (1991) investigated concordance rates for schizophrenia for people who were related in various ways. The concordance rate was found to be greater for MZ twins (48%) than for DZ twins (17%), suggesting that the disorder has a genetic basis.

Although twin studies of schizophrenia show higher concordance rates for MZ twin pairs than for DZ twin pairs, no studies show a concordance rate of 100% for MZ twins. This means that other factors, like environment and experience, must also be responsible. It is now widely thought that we have a genetic pre-disposition to schizophrenia, which is probably triggered by stressful experience.

Strengths of twin studies

- Twins are ideally suited to the investigation of genetic influences, offering an opportunity for a natural matched-pairs experiment.
- More recent twin studies are well controlled.

Limitations of twin studies

- MZ twins raised together are treated more alike than DZ twins raised together. This means that it is difficult to separate out the effect of genes from the effects of the environment.

- In early studies, twins said to have been raised apart were often not entirely separated; they often attended the same school and saw each other regularly.
- Truly separated twins are rare, so most studies use small samples.

Family and adoption studies

Children share genetic material with their biological parents. Adopted children, however, do not share any genetic material with their adopted parents. Adoption studies usually involve comparing a trait or characteristic between adopted children and both their biological and adoptive parents. If a trait is genetic, there should be more similarity between the adopted child and the biological parents. If a trait is not genetic, there should be greater similarity between the adopted child and the adoptive parents. Another form of adoption study might investigate the similarity between parents and their children, one adopted and one biological. Adoption studies tend to offer strong evidence for genetic influences, but they often involve small samples; it is important to use children who were adopted when they were very young.

Study

Kety (1988) investigated schizophrenia in 5000 people who had been adopted in early life. Of these, 33 were found to suffer from schizophrenia as adults. Kety then looked at both the biological and adoptive parents. Fourteen percent of the biological parents were found to have been diagnosed with schizophrenia, compared to only 2.7% of the adoptive parents. This study supports the view that schizophrenia has a genetic basis.

Study

Scarr and Weinberg (1978) compared the intelligence test results of parents with those of their biological and adopted children. There was a higher degree of similarity between the abilities of parents and their biological children than between parents and their adopted children. The findings suggest that intelligence has a genetic rather than environmental basis.

Gender development
Concepts

Specification content

Sex and gender: androgyny; sex-role stereotypes; cultural variations in gender-related behaviour; nature and nurture.

Sex and gender

Sex is a biological term referring to our status as either male or female. It is determined by chromosomes, hormones and anatomical differences.

Gender is a psychosocial term referring to the roles, attitudes and behaviours associated with being either male or female. These differ according to the society in which we live, making gender a **social construction**.

Related terms include **masculine** and **feminine.** Masculine behaviours, roles and attitudes are those thought to be appropriate for males. Feminine behaviours, roles and attitudes are those thought to be appropriate for females.

Androgyny is a term meaning the possession of both masculine and feminine characteristics. It has been proposed that androgynous people are more psychologically healthy than people who are either strongly masculine or strongly feminine.

Bem's sex-role inventory (BSRI) (1974) measures androgyny. To complete the BSRI, respondents have to rate themselves on a 7-point scale for a list of traits such as warm, gentle, forceful and aggressive. After completing the questionnaire, an overall masculinity score and an overall femininity score can be calculated. This allows the respondent to plot themselves on the two dimensions.

Evaluation

- Other researchers argue that a high masculinity score is important for psychological well-being rather than a mixture of masculine and feminine traits.
- Reducing complicated concepts to a single score based on a list of traits is an oversimplification. More recently, researchers have measured other aspects of gender, like hobbies and abilities, rather than just personality characteristics.
- The BSRI was developed using American students' views of what was desirable in men and women in the 1970s.
- The BSRI produces similar results if repeated with the same sample, so it is reliable.

Sex-role or gender stereotypes

A sex-role stereotype or gender stereotype is a fixed belief about what we expect of males and females. It can include beliefs about behaviours, attitudes and traits. For example, according to traditional gender stereotypes, males are expected to be good at practical things like putting up shelves, to enjoy sport and be brave. In contrast, females are expected to be good at looking after children, to enjoy shopping and be gentle.

Study

Seavey, Katz and Zalk (1975) studied how adults reacted to a baby that they thought was either male or female. Adult participants were left with a 3-month-old baby dressed in a yellow baby outfit for 3 minutes. Available toys included a ball, a rag doll and a plastic ring. When told the child was female, participants tended to give the child the doll, but when told the baby was male, they tended to give the baby the plastic ring. The researchers concluded that adults behave differently towards babies according to what sex they think the babies are. This is an example of what is known as a 'Baby X' study. In general, experiments like this show that how a baby is labelled, as either male or female, affects the way the infant is treated and played with.

Study

Urberg (1982) investigated children's gender stereotypes. 3-, 5- and 7-year-olds heard stories in which characters whose sex was unspecified showed traits such as gentleness or bravery. The children were then asked who would show the trait in the story, whether it would be a woman, a man, or neither. They found that all children answered according to gender stereotypes, showing that children have clear beliefs about the characteristics and behaviours typical of males and females.

Cultural variations in gender-related behaviour

Mead (1935) studied differences in gender roles in three different societies in New Guinea. She found that there were cultural differences in gender-related behaviour. Males and females in the Arapesh society were gentle and cooperative, behaving in a typically feminine way. Males and females in the Mundugamor society behaved in a typically male, aggressive way. Males and females in the Tchambuli society had distinct gender roles that were the opposite of traditional Western sex roles. This is an example of a cross-cultural study, comparing the behaviours and attitudes shown in different cultures. Any differences found to exist between cultures are then assumed to be due to differences in socialisation and experience.

Evaluation

- Mead's methods have been criticised for being unscientific.
- Mead may have been biased. She expected to find cultural differences and this expectation perhaps affected her observations.
- Mead later changed her ideas about the extent to which culture influences gender and suggested that women were 'naturally' better at caring for children than men.
- Mead has been accused of exaggerating cultural differences in gender-related behaviour.
- The general notion of cultural differences in gender-related behaviour may be correct; Wade and Tavris (1998) reported cultural differences: for example, the status of women is relatively high in Scandinavian countries and very low in Bangladesh.

Nature and nurture

The nature–nurture debate is concerned with the relative importance of the influences of biology and the environment on our behaviour. According to the **nature** view, gender is predominantly the result of biological factors such as genes and hormones. According to the **nurture** view, gender is predominantly the result of environmental factors such as family, education and life experiences. The mid-point in the debate would be the **interactionist** view that both nature and nurture contribute to gender. In any discussion of the nature–nurture debate in relation to gender, it is important to refer to explanations of gender, in particular, the explanations offered by biological and social learning theory.

Explaining gender development

Specification content

Biological explanations: typical and atypical sex chromosomes; androgens and oestrogens. Social learning theory: reinforcement; modelling; imitation and identification. Cognitive approach: Kohlberg's cognitive developmental theory including gender identity, stability and constancy; gender schema theory. Psychodynamic approach: Freud's psychoanalytic theory; Oedipus complex; Electra complex; identification.

Biological explanations of gender

Biological psychologists explain gender in terms of:

- chromosomes
- brain structure
- hormones

Typical sex chromosome patterns

Biological sex is determined by the combination of chromosomes for the 23rd chromosome pair.

For males, the typical sex chromosome pattern is XY. For females, the typical sex chromosome pattern is XX.

Atypical sex chromosome patterns

A condition known as **Klinefelter's syndrome** involves the presence of an extra X chromosome, giving a combination of XXY. Klinefelter's syndrome occurs in between one in 500 and one in 1000 males. People with Klinefelter's syndrome are biological males. They tend to behave passively in relation to most males, have poor language skills and are infertile. Physically tall, their legs are long in relation to the torso.

The condition **Turner's syndrome** occurs in females who have only one X chromosome, resulting in the combination XO. Turner's syndrome affects one in 2500 females. People with Turner's syndrome are biological females. They usually have good verbal ability and poor visual–spatial ability. They have no functioning ovaries and usually have a short and squat physique.

Studying the psychological effects of atypical sex chromosome patterns allows us to make inferences about the effects of male and female chromosomes on psychological functioning in people with typical sex chromosome combinations.

Study

The case of the Batista boys shows how chromosomal constitution can be more important for gender identity than how we are raised. Imperato-McGinley (1979) studied boys in a family with a genetic abnormality. The boys appeared female at birth and were brought up as females. However, because of a genetic mutation, they changed into boys at puberty. Their chromosome pattern was always XY (that of a normal male). Despite having been treated for years as girls, these boys adjusted well to their male identity showing how biology can over-ride socialisation.

Study

The case of Bruce Reimer (Money and Erhardt 1972) showed how socialisation cannot overcome biology. Bruce lost his penis in a routine operation when he was a baby. His parents were advised to bring him up as a girl. Bruce had gender re-assignment surgery and was given the female hormone oestrogen at puberty. Despite years of being socialised as a female, Bruce eventually rejected the female role and reverted to being male. He stopped the oestrogen treatment and later had further surgery to restore his male appearance. The case suggests that biological influences (XY chromosomes) are more important than socialisation.

Evaluation

■ Both cases are unusual and may not therefore tell us much about normal gender development.

Brain structure

Perhaps brain differences between males and females affect gender-related behaviour. Gorski et al. (1978) discovered that a region of the hypothalamus known as the **sexually dimorphic nucleus** is larger in male rats than in female rats. This difference is thought to be due to the action of the male hormone testosterone.

Hormones: testosterone and oestrogen

Hormones are chemicals that are secreted by glands.

Testosterone is a male hormone (androgen). It determines the development of male sex organs and has been found to have behavioural effects.

- The condition congenital adrenal hyperplasia (CAH) causes high levels of male hormones in both males and females. In females, CAH has been said to result in increased aggression, preference for male toys and an increased spatial ability. However, not all studies of CAH girls show these effects.
- Animal research using rats tends to show that increasing testosterone levels causes increases in aggression.
- Body builders taking androgen steroids have been found to show higher than normal aggression scores using aggression questionnaires. However, this may have been due to other factors such as occupation. Experimental research has shown no significant differences in anger and aggression between participants taking testosterone substances and controls (Tricker et al. 1996).
- Prison research has shown links between high testosterone levels and aggressive behaviour (Dabbs et al. 1995).

Oestrogen is a female hormone that determines female sexual characteristics and menstruation. It may also have psychological and behavioural effects.

Pre-menstrual syndrome (PMS), or pre-menstrual tension (PMT), can lead to moodiness, depression, aggression and irritable behaviour. PMT has been blamed for antisocial behaviour, such as shoplifting, and even for extreme violent acts such as murder. Research has not found any consistent evidence that oestrogen is responsible for the psychological symptoms that many women report (Golombok and Fivush, 1994).

- Some evidence suggests that biological factors affect gender-related behaviour.
- Most studies do not allow us to infer cause and effect. Maybe differences in brain structure and hormones are a result of being male or female rather than a cause of male or female behaviour.
- Biological explanations cannot explain individual differences in gender-related behaviour.
- Environmental influences should also be considered.
- Contrast the biological view with that of social learning theorists.

Social learning theory of gender

Social learning theory would suggest that gender is learned through observation and imitation. Key social learning theory concepts are described below.

Imitation

Imitation is simply copying behaviour.

Reinforcement

Positive reinforcement is when we receive something pleasant for the performance of a behaviour. Positive reinforcement acts like a reward, strengthening the learned behaviour and making it more likely to be produced again in the future. Sometimes we learn through observing the consequences for others of their behaviour. This is known as **vicarious reinforcement**. Quite a lot of evidence seems to show that boys and girls are reinforced for different behaviours.

Study

Fagot (1978) observed 24 young children at home playing with their parents. She found that parents reinforced girls for asking for help, playing close by and dressing up. Boys, on the other hand, were reinforced for playing with building bricks and were actively discouraged from doll play.

Study

Smith and Lloyd (1978) showed that mothers would treat an infant differently according to the gender they believed it to be. If told it was a boy, they would give it a hammer to play with and engage in rough activity like bouncing. If told it was a girl, they would give it a doll and behave in a more calm and soothing manner.

Identification

Identification involves the child wanting to be like a specific person and results in close observation and imitation of that person's behaviour and mannerisms.

Modelling

Modelling is the process of copying a chosen person's behaviour. The usual role model for a boy is the father, and for a girl, the mother. Children may have several models whose behaviour they try to imitate.

Social learning theorists noted that observation of someone's behaviour is not on its own sufficient to lead to imitation. They understood that **cognitive factors** affect whether or not modelling takes place. Two such cognitive factors are similarity and appropriateness.

- **Similarity** — children have been found to be more likely to imitate same-sex models. Perry and Bussey (1979) showed how female children are more likely to copy female adults, and male children are more likely to copy male adults.
- **Appropriateness** — Masters et al. (1979) showed how boys and girls were likely to copy toy choices shown by their own sex only if they were also told that the toy was appropriate for their sex. If they were told that the toy was appropriate for the other sex, then they would not choose it, despite what they had seen.

Evaluation

- Studies show that boys and girls are treated and reinforced differently.
- Cross-cultural studies (e.g. Mead) indicate that gender is socially constructed.
- The theory recognises that cognitive factors affect learning.
- Many studies of modelling have low ecological validity; they involve the use of adult strangers as models or use videos; the models are carrying out artificial behaviours in an artificial context.
- The theory does not explain why gender develops gradually over years.
- There is no explanation for why two boys or two girls who have been brought up by the same parents show different gender identities. For example, one boy may be rough and tough whilst his brother is more gentle and caring.
- The theory assumes that biology has little effect on gender development.

Cognitive approach to gender

The cognitive approach is concerned with how the child understands gender rather than the source of gender identity.

Kohlberg's cognitive developmental theory

Kohlberg suggested that a child's understanding of gender develops in a series of increasingly sophisticated stages.

- **Gender identity** At the age of 2–3 years, a child can label his/her own sex and label other people as male or female.
- **Gender stability** At the age of 3–4 years, a child realises that sex stays the same over time. However, children in this stage do not understand that gender stays the same across situations. For example, a child might think that a girl has changed into a boy because she is playing with a car. Children in this stage are also easily fooled by external appearance, for example, believing that a man who has long hair is really a woman.
- **Gender constancy (consistency)** Between the ages of $4\frac{1}{2}$ and 7 years, children acquire a full understanding of gender, knowing that gender stays the same across time, in different situations and despite changes in outward appearance.

Study

Slaby and Frey (1975) interviewed young children using a series of questions. For example, asking whether a doll or person in a photograph was male or female. This question assessed understanding of gender identity. To test gender stability, the children were asked what sex they would be when they grew up. To test gender constancy, children were asked whether or not they would be a girl or a boy if they wore opposite-sex clothes or played with opposite-sex toys. Answers to these questions confirmed the stages described by Kohlberg.

Research using other methods has confirmed that thoughts about gender may change with age. For example, Damon (1977) asked children questions about a boy called George who wanted to play with dolls and wear a dress to school. At different ages children's responses to this scenario were quite different. Four-year-olds thought it was alright for George to play with dolls; 6-year-olds had very fixed views that it was unacceptable; older children thought it was unusual, but not necessarily wrong.

Evaluation

- There is cross-cultural support for Kohlberg's three stages.
- Kohlberg's theory describes the sequence of gender development but does not explain the cause of gender development.

Gender schema theory

A **gender schema** is a unit of knowledge consisting of information such as appropriate behaviours, characteristics, occupations and roles for males and females (Martin and Halverson 1981). Initially, a child identifies what activities and toys are appropriate for his or her sex. A child then actively seeks out further own-gender information leading to the development of more complex gender schemas. Martin and Halverson (1981) propose three stages in the development of gender schemas:

- Learning what attitudes and behaviours are usually associated with each sex.
- Making links between different aspects of the schema for one's own sex. For example, knowing that if someone plays with cars, that person is also likely to wear trousers and have short hair.
- Making these links for gender schemas for both sexes.

Studies show that young children are more aware of own-sex activities than opposite-sex activities. For example, Boston and Levy (1991) found that young children were able to outline typically male or female activities more accurately for their own-gender activity than for the opposite-gender activity. It has also been found that children reject or misremember information that conflicts with their gender schema. Cordua et al. (1979) showed that young children remembered sex-stereotypical video content quite accurately, but misremembered the content of videos with non-sex-stereotyped content. For example, they might misremember that a doctor character was a man, even though in the video the doctor character was female.

Evaluation

- According to gender schema theory, children identify with their own sex sooner than Kohlberg suggested.
- The theory explains why children do not automatically copy a same-sex model, but first look to see whether the behaviour is appropriate.
- Boys have been found to show more extreme gender-typed behaviour than girls, which gender schema theory cannot explain.
- Cognitive theories state that gender understanding begins around 2 years of age, which does not explain why children choose to play with those of the same sex before this age.
- Cognitive theories take little account of the role of social interaction in the development of gender, assuming that the process is largely passive.

Psychodynamic approach to gender

Freud's psychoanalytic theory of gender

Freud's theory of development proposed that development takes place in psycho-sexual stages; at each stage the child experiences an unconscious conflict. Gender development takes place during the **phallic stage** at about 5 years. In this stage, the child's libido or psychic energy is directed towards the genital area and gender identity develops through the resolution of either the Oedipus complex (boys) or the Electra complex (girls).

Oedipus complex

The boy develops a desire for his mother; at the same time he is afraid of his father who he sees as a powerful rival for the mother's affection. Fearing the father's revenge, the boy becomes anxious that his father will castrate him. To resolve this conflicting desire between love for his mother and fear of castration, the boy gives up the love for his mother and identifies with his father. Freud refers to this as **identification with the aggressor**. Through this identification the boy adopts the father's male identity and assumes male characteristics. According to Freud's theory, a boy who has not resolved his Oedipus complex will be confused about his sexual identity.

Electra complex

The girl realises that she lacks a penis and thinks that she has already been castrated. The girl blames the mother. She develops **penis envy**, which leads to desire for the father who possesses what she wants. Unable to have a penis of her own, her 'penis envy' is converted into a desire for a baby (the 'penis-baby' project). In this way, the girl identifies with the mother and assumes the female role and female characteristics.

Freud saw female identification as being weaker than male identification because girls believe they have already suffered castration, so are therefore much less fearful than boys. This would suggest therefore that boys actively identify with the father, whereas for girls, the process is more passive. This active–passive difference can be seen in the gender roles as they develop, with boys becoming active, dominant and aggressive, and girls becoming quiet, passive and submissive.

Study

The case of **Little Hans** is often used to illustrate the Oedipus complex. At the age of 4 years, Hans developed a phobia of being bitten by a horse. Hans's father, who was a friend of Freud, wrote to Freud about his child's phobia asking for his opinion. Hans particularly feared white horses with black blinkers and black mouths. Freud suggested that Hans had an unconscious fear of his father, and that the horse was merely a symbol of the father who had a beard and wore glasses. Hans's fear of being bitten symbolised his fear of being castrated by his father. According to Freud's analysis, Hans was a little Oedipus.

Evaluation

- Hans's phobia may be better explained through classical conditioning; his fear had developed as a result of him seeing a frightening accident involving a horse.
- Freud's theory assumes that children who grow up in a household without both mother and father would have sex-role identification problems, but studies have found that children living in such 'atypical' households show traditional gender roles.
- Gender identity does not develop suddenly at the age of 4 or 5 years as Freud's theory would predict. In fact, most children show gender awareness well before that age.
- There is little or no empirical evidence to support psychodynamic theory.
- The notion of childhood sexuality is controversial.

Neo-Freudians (new Freudians) have developed Freud's ideas in their own views about gender. **Karen Horney** proposes that penis envy is really a desire for the power and control that males possess in society. **Erik Erikson** suggests that females do not experience penis envy and that men are actually envious of women's ability to create. **Nancy Chodorow** suggests that gender identity is based on the early mother–child relationship. Mothers identify more strongly with daughters than sons, encouraging greater closeness with daughters. As a result, female children identify via the mother with the female role and male children are encouraged to be separate and reject femininity.

Research methods

Planning research

Specification content

Qualitative and quantitative research and data collection techniques. Formulating research questions: stating aims; formulating hypotheses (null/experimental/alternative/research). Populations and sampling: sampling techniques, including opportunity, random, stratified and systematic.

Qualitative and quantitative research

Qualitative research focuses on thoughts and feelings and usually involves some form of interview or an observation. Qualitative data are meaningful information because they are usually collected first-hand and the information can be put into context. **Quantitative research** focuses on numerical data. Data collected in quantitative research are less meaningful because the information is narrowly focused (e.g. score in a memory test) and is taken out of context. Qualitative data can be converted into quantitative data, e.g by categorising responses in an interview and then calculating frequencies of certain types of response.

Formulating research questions

Most research stems from other studies or arises because a researcher wants to investigate the validity of a theory. Research questions can also arise when there is a problem to be solved, e.g. where a researcher wants to test the effectiveness of a new treatment.

Stating aims

The aim of an investigation states what it is the researcher is trying to find out. The aim need not be testable but should give a clear idea of what is involved.

Formulating hypotheses

The next job is for the researcher to formulate a precise testable statement — the hypothesis. A hypothesis predicts the relationship between two variables. A good hypothesis should specify clearly what the conditions of the experiment are and what exactly is to be measured.

The **research** or **alternative hypothesis (H1)** predicts that an effect will occur. This is sometimes referred to as an **experimental hypothesis** if the research method used is an experiment. The **null hypothesis (H0)** predicts that the expected effect will not occur. The null hypothesis is not the opposite of the research hypothesis, it just states that there will be no effect. After analysing the data the researcher either accepts the H0 and rejects the H1 (there is no effect); or rejects the H0 and accepts the H1 (there is an effect). Defining variables clearly in the hypothesis is known as **operationalisation**.

- *Incorrect H1:* *'People's memory will be better if information is organised.'*
- *Correct H1:* *'People will recall more words from a list when the words are presented in categorised groups than when they are presented randomly.'*
- *Correct corresponding H0:* *'There will be no difference in the number of words recalled whether the words are presented in categorised groups or presented randomly.'*

Populations and sampling

The term **sample** refers to the people (participants) who take part in research. The larger group of people from whom the sample is chosen is the **target population**. It is important that the sample represents the population so that the results can be generalised to a wider group of people than just those that have been studied. **Sampling bias** can occur where the sample is dominated by a particular sub-group in the target population, for example, mostly males.

Sampling techniques

Opportunity sample: people who are easily available.

> **Strength**

- This method is quick and easy.

> **Limitation**

- **Researcher bias** may occur where the researcher chooses whoever he or she wants to take part. The participants may be a group of similar people, even the researcher's friends; the sample is unlikely to be representative, making it difficult to generalise.

Random sample: every member of the target population has an equal chance of being chosen. This can be done by drawing names from a hat or by giving everyone a number and using a computer programme to generate random numbers.

> **Strength**

- No researcher bias as the researcher does not control who is chosen.

> **Limitation**

- The sample may still not be representative; by chance there might be more males in the sample than females.

Stratified sample: the researcher randomly selects participants from different sub-groups (strata) within the population. Each sub-group is represented proportionately. For example, if the target population includes 100 males and 200 females then the sample should have one male for every two females.

> **Strength**

- It is likely to give a representative sample.

> **Limitation**

- It is sometimes difficult to identify the sub-groups. It is also time-consuming.

Systematic sample: every *n*th member of the target population is selected, for example, every third employee on a payroll.

> **Strength**

- No researcher bias.

> **Limitation**

- The sample may not necessarily be representative.

Experimental methods

Specification content

Field, laboratory and quasi-experiments; ecological validity. Independent and dependent variables. Extraneous and confounding variables. Experimental designs: repeated, matched and independent. Controls including counterbalancing.

Field, laboratory and quasi-experiments

In an experiment one variable is changed or manipulated and the effect on another variable is measured. The variable that the researcher manipulates is the **independent variable (IV)**, and the variable the researcher measures is the **dependent variable (DV)**. All other variables should be controlled. This control allows the researcher to make assumptions about a cause-and-effect relationship between the IV and the DV.

Field experiment

A field experiment takes place in a natural environment. Field experiments are high in **ecological validity** because they involve the study of behaviour in a real-life situation. A good example is Bickman's research (1974), where people were asked to pick up litter by someone dressed either in ordinary clothes or in a uniform.

Laboratory experiment

Laboratory experiments take place in a constant environment with external variables such as noise and distractions controlled; so each participant performs in exactly the same conditions. Laboratory experiments can result in artificial behaviour because people behave differently when they know they are being studied. In addition, experimental tasks are often highly artificial. As a result, laboratory experiments may lack **ecological validity**.

Quasi-experiment

In quasi-experiments there is no random allocation to conditions and no directly controlled manipulation of the IV. This would occur when an experimenter compares the performance of two different groups of people, for example, males and females. In quasi-experiments the researcher cannot draw such clear conclusions about cause and effect as in experiments in which there is direct manipulation of the IV.

Independent and dependent variables

The **independent variable (IV)** is the variable the researcher manipulates. The **dependent variable (DV)** is the variable the researcher measures. Using the example of recall for a list of words that are either organised into categories or randomly presented, the IV would be whether or not the words are categorised, and the DV would be the number of words recalled. When you have to identify the IV and DV in a study, first decide what the researcher is measuring — this is the DV. The other variable that changes must therefore be the IV.

> **IV and DV examples**
> **An experiment to see whether people will wait longer in a queue if music is playing or not**
>
> IV   whether music is playing or not
>
> DV waiting time in minutes

> **An experiment to see whether people who do crosswords more than twice a week score more highly in a spelling test than people who do not**
>
> IV whether people do crosswords more than twice a week or not
>
> DV spelling test score

Extraneous and confounding variables: control

An **extraneous variable** is any variable, other than the independent variable, that might affect the dependent variable. An extraneous variable needs to be controlled by the researcher so that it does not become a **confounding variable**, spoiling the results of the study. If results are confounded by an uncontrolled extraneous variable, then we cannot say that the IV has affected the DV and so cannot draw sensible conclusions.

Examples of extraneous variables that should be controlled are: time allowed for completion of a task; outside noise; presence of other people; use of different materials in each condition; different experimenters for each condition; variations in wording of instructions.

Where the experimenter knowingly or unknowingly treats different participants differently, this is known as **experimenter bias**. To control for experimenter bias it is sensible to use written **standardised instructions** so that each participant has the same experience during the experiment. Another strategy for coping with experimenter bias is to carry out **double-blind research**, where the researcher who actually carries out the experiment does not know the aim of the research.

Experimental designs

There are three experimental designs in psychological research.

> ### Repeated or related measures design
> The same people are used in both conditions and their performances are compared.
>
> #### Strengths
> - There are no **individual differences** or **participant variables**.
> - Fewer participants are needed overall.
>
> #### Limitations
> - **Order effects** may occur, i.e. participants' performance in the second condition may be affected by their experience of the first condition. They may improve their performance in the second condition because they have had a practice (**practice effect**); or they may be worse in the second condition because they are tired or bored (**fatigue effect**). To control for order effects the researcher should **counterbalance** the conditions, with half the participants doing Condition A then B, and the other half doing Condition B and then A.

- Participants may guess what the study is about and may behave differently than if they had not known.
- Different sets of materials may be required.

Independent groups design

Different participants perform in each condition and their performances are compared. Here it is important to randomly allocate participants to the conditions to avoid researcher bias. **Random allocation** means that everyone has an equal chance of being in either condition. It can be done by drawing names out of a hat.

Strengths

- No order effects.
- Participants cannot guess the purpose of the study.
- Only one set of stimulus materials is required.

Limitations

- Individual differences or participant variables may affect the results.
- More participants are needed overall.

Matched pairs design

Different people perform in each condition, but they are matched in ways that matter for the experiment, for example, sex, age and IQ. For each participant in Condition A, there must be a matching participant in the other condition.

Strengths

- Individual differences or participant variables are reduced.
- There are no order effects.
- Participants cannot guess the purpose of the study.
- Only one set of materials is needed.

Limitations

- It is difficult and time-consuming to match pairs.
- No two people are exactly the same. Therefore matching cannot eliminate individual differences altogether.

Strengths of the experimental method

- A **cause-and-effect relationship** between the IV and DV can be determined.
- Strictly controlled procedures mean that **replication** is possible to check whether the findings are **reliable**.
- It is more ethical than methods where participants are unaware that they are being studied.
- Measures are **objective**, that is, can be directly observed.

- Experiments often lack ecological validity because they test behaviour in a way in which it might not occur in real life.
- Participants may pick up clues as to the purpose of the experiment and respond to these **demand characteristics** by behaving differently to how they would normally behave. Some participants try to 'make the experiment work'; others might try to 'mess the experiment up'.

Non-experimental methods

Specification content

Self-report methods: questionnaire construction; types of interviews. Correlation studies; the difference between experiments and correlations. Observational studies. Content analysis. Case studies. Pilot studies.

Self-report methods

This is where participants report on their own behaviour, feelings or opinions. Self-report methods are often described as **subjective** because they are based on the participant's opinion. Questionnaires and interviews are both examples of self-report methods.

Questionnaires

Questionnaires are used to study behaviours and attitudes that cannot be directly observed. Questionnaire items should be clear and unambiguous.

Closed questions: there are a fixed number of optional answers.

Example: Do you think that cannabis should be legalised?

        YES   NO   DON'T KNOW

Closed questions give data that are easy to analyse. Answers, however, may have low validity because people cannot give their own answer, and instead have to go for the nearest option.

Open questions: respondents can put any answer they like.

Example: How much alcohol do you drink per week on average?

Open questions give more meaningful and valid information as people can put the answer they want, but the data are difficult to analyse.

- Data can be collected quickly.
- The method can be replicated.
- There are no ethical problems as participants know they are taking part.

Limitations of the questionnaire method

- It is difficult to construct a good questionnaire.
- Social desirability — respondents try to make themselves appear to be 'nice'.
- 'Yeh' saying — a bias towards agreement on questionnaires.
- Response set — people just choose all 'yes' or all 'no' answers.

Interviews

Structured interview: pre-prepared questions are asked in a fixed order. If each participant answers the same questions, the data can be analysed easily and the interview stays focused. However, in a structured interview there is no chance to ask any extra questions if an interesting issue arises during the interview.

Unstructured interview: there is an aim but no fixed questions; the researcher can ask any questions that are appropriate. Unstructured interviews produce more detailed and valid data, but responses are all different and therefore difficult to analyse and the interview may go off track.

Strengths of the interview method

- It is useful for the study of opinions and past experiences.
- It produces many data.

Limitations of the interview method

- It is a self-report method and therefore subjective.
- It tells us little about the causes of behaviour.
- The interviewer's personality and style are likely to affect the outcome.

Correlation studies

Correlation is a statistical technique used to measure the relationship between two variables. Correlations are usually represented in the form of a scattergram.

In a **positive correlation** (see Figure 4), as one variable increases the other variable increases. In a **negative correlation,** as one variable increases, the other variable decreases.

Correlations allow us to make predictions: for example, if we know there is a positive correlation between number of days' holiday and happiness, then we could predict that someone who has lots of holidays will be happier and vice versa.

Strengths of the correlation method

- Correlations show a relationship.
- Correlations enable predictions about behaviour.

Limitations of the correlation method

- Correlations do not tell us that one variable causes another — they do not show cause and effect.

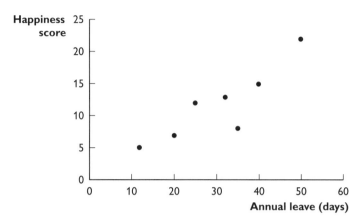

Figure 4 Scattergram to show the relationship between the number of days of annual holiday and happiness score

Key differences between an experiment and a correlation study

Experiment: control of extraneous variables; shows cause and effect.

Correlation: no control of extraneous variables; does not show cause and effect.

Observational studies

In a **natural observation**, observations take place in a natural environment, for example in a playground or at a football match. Extraneous variables are not controlled, but there is high validity because the behaviour is real behaviour in a real setting. **Controlled observations** are conducted under controlled conditions with extraneous variables eliminated. This control allows for replication, but it means the data may have less validity because the situation is artificial.

In a **participant observation** the observer joins in the action with those being observed, allowing behaviour to be understood in context. Participant observation can result in loss of objectivity because the observer is too involved in what is going on. The observer's presence may also affect the outcome. In **non-participant observation**, the observer merely watches and does not take part, allowing the observer to be more objective.

In a **overt observation** people know that they are being observed. This is ethical but may lead to artificial behaviour if people know that they are being watched. This is known as an **observer effect**. **Covert observation** is where people do not know they are being observed. This avoids an **observer effect**, but could be unethical because people have not given their consent.

Observational recording techniques

Observational researchers often use a category system, breaking down the target behaviour into operational categories. For example, if the target behaviour is 'aggression', the **behavioural categories** might be hitting, smacking, kicking, hair-pulling. To be useful, category systems should be clear and unambiguous. Any instances of these behaviours can be recorded on a tally chart.

Observers may make **continuous recordings,** noting down every instance of the target behaviour as it occurs. Continuous recording is appropriate where the target behaviour occurs as a separate event (e.g. a hit or a smack), but is not suitable for recording behaviours that are on-going (e.g. playing with another child). For such behaviours, **time sampling** is a useful technique. Here the total observation time is divided into time intervals (e.g. every minute), and at each time interval the behaviour is noted.

Observer bias is where the researcher's beliefs or expectations lead them to be biased in their observations. For example, if a researcher expects boys to be more aggressive than girls, this could affect the way an action is interpreted during the observation. To avoid this bias two researchers often observe side by side but record separately. Ideally, both sets of observations should be the same. This is known as **inter-observer reliability**.

Strengths of the observational method
- Data have high ecological validity.
- It is useful for studying social behaviours.

Limitations of the observational method
- There may be observer bias.
- There may be an observer effect.
- It does not show cause and effect (unless part of an experiment).
- It is time-consuming.
- Ethical problems — lack of consent, lack of right to withdraw, invasion of privacy.

Content analysis

Content analysis involves systematic measurement of aspects of media communications, such as books and television programmes. Various units can be analysed, e.g. number of male/female characters, words, ideas. The data are usually recorded in the form of frequencies.

Strengths of content analysis method
- It is appropriate for any form of media.
- There are no ethical problems.

Limitations of content analysis method
- Behaviour is being studied out of context. For example, studying the content of a politician's speech does not take account of the mood of the audience.
- Categories are decided in advance and are based on the researcher's expectations.
- Interpretation may be subjective.

Case studies

Case studies are usually conducted by clinical psychologists and involve in-depth research with a single person or a small group. Several forms of data can be used including observations, interviews, psychological testing etc. Medical and school history records might also be useful depending on the situation. The psychologist produces a description of the case, followed by an interpretation of the findings. In clinical cases there might also be some recommendation for future treatment.

Strengths of the case study method

- The data are rich in detail.
- It enables a long-term view.
- It has high validity because the research is based on a real person and his or her real experiences.
- A single case can be used to challenge theory.

Limitations of the case study method

- Results cannot be generalised.
- Often based on recall, which may not be reliable.
- The researcher's expectations may affect their interpretation — **researcher bias**.
- Ethical issues such as consent, right to withdraw, protection from harm and confidentiality need to be carefully considered.

Pilot studies

A pilot study is a small-scale investigation carried out as a preliminary to the main investigation. The pilot study allows the researcher to determine whether there are any problems with the design or materials so that adjustments can be made before carrying out the full-scale investigation. Pilot studies can be used for any type of investigation: an experimental procedure can be trialled with a couple of participants to see that they understand the standardised instructions; a questionnaire can be trialled with a few respondents to see whether they understand the wording of the questions; a researcher may carry out a pilot observation to see whether or not categories are appropriate.

Representing data and descriptive statistics

Specification content

Calculation and use of measures of central tendency (mean, median and mode) and measures of dispersion (range and standard deviation). Correlation as a description of the relationship between two variables. Positive, negative and zero correlations. Appropriate use of tabular and graphical displays: tables, bar charts, histograms, graphs, scattergrams.

Descriptive statistics

In an examination you may be asked to perform simple calculations so you need to know how to calculate the mean, median, mode and range. It is unlikely that you would be asked to calculate the standard deviation in an examination, but you need to know what the SD means and how it differs from the range.

Measures of central tendency

A measure of central tendency is a single figure that is used to show an average score for a set of scores.

There are three measures of central tendency:
- the mean
- the median
- the mode

To calculate **the mean** ($\bar{x}$) add up all the scores and divide by the number of scores. The mean is very sensitive because it uses all the scores, but it can be distorted by an extreme or **anomalous** score.

The median is the middle score when all the scores have been put into order from lowest to highest. If there is no middle score, add together the two middle scores and divide by two. The median is not distorted by extreme scores, but is not as sensitive as the mean because not all scores are used in the calculation.

The mode is simply the most frequent score in a set of scores. It is easy to find but is a very crude measure and not very useful: for example, there may be more than one mode or there may not be one at all.

Measures of dispersion

As well as finding an average score, it is important to know how much spread there is in a set of scores. Two measures of dispersion or spread are:
- the range
- the standard deviation

To find the **range,** subtract the lowest score from the highest score. The range can be distorted by an extremely high or low score, leading us to believe that a set of scores is spread out — even when the majority of the scores are close to the mean.

The **standard deviation (SD)** takes account of every score in a set of scores, thus representing the spread for the scores as a whole. A low SD means that the scores are not spread out, whereas a high SD means the scores are widely spread. The calculation for the SD takes into account the distance of each score from the mean and is much more sensitive than the range.

> **Procedure for calculating the SD**
> **(1)** Find the mean for the set of scores.
> **(2)** Subtract each score from the mean.
> **(3)** Square the answers to step 2 above.
> **(4)** Add up the answers to step 3 above.
> **(5)** Divide the answer to step 4 above by the total number of scores minus 1.
> **(6)** Find the square root of step 5 above.

Representing data

You will need to be familiar with the different methods of representing data and should be prepared to sketch simple graphs and tables in the examination. Remember that, in the examination, marks are awarded for axis labels and titles as well as for plotting the graphs.

Tabular displays: summary tables

Tables should have a clear title and column headings. The title must refer to the two conditions by name and include the unit of measurement (i.e. what the numbers refer to).

	Males	Females
Average weekly ice-cream consumption (ml)	60	180

Average weekly ice-cream consumption (in millilitres) for males and females

Also be prepared to write a short verbal summary: 'Notice from the above table that females, on average, consume more ice-cream in a week than males'.

Graphical displays
- bar charts
- histograms
- line graphs
- scattergrams

Bar charts are used to show frequencies in columns with the frequency on the vertical axis and the variable on the horizontal axis. The bar chart shown in Figure 5 illustrates the information about ice-cream consumption shown in the table.

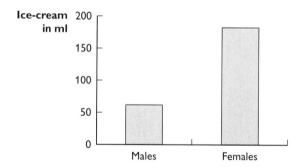

Figure 5 Average weekly ice-cream consumption (in millilitres) for males and females

Histograms are used to display continuous data where the variable being measured is in equal intervals, e.g. years. The intervals normally appear on the horizontal axis and the frequency on the vertical axis. Histograms usually appear as columns, but the midpoints of each column can be joined to produce a frequency polygon. The histogram shown in Figure 6 depicts the number of participants and their scores in a memory test.

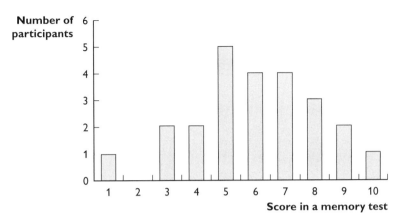

Figure 6 Number of participants and their scores in a memory test

Line graphs show a relationship between independent and dependent variables, with the IV on the horizontal axis and the DV on the vertical axis. A line graph is only appropriate where the variable is continuous. Contrast this with the bar graph of means; it would not be meaningful to join the means for males and females as they are quite separate. The line graph in Figure 7 shows the average ice-cream consumption (ml) for males in the months March to November.

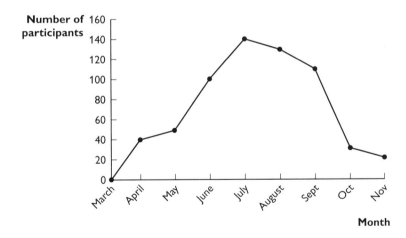

Figure 7 Average ice-cream consumption (ml) for males from March to November

Scattergrams are used for correlational data. One variable is plotted on each axis with each pair shown as a single cross on the scattergram. The pattern of crosses indicates a positive, negative or zero correlation, as shown in Figure 8.

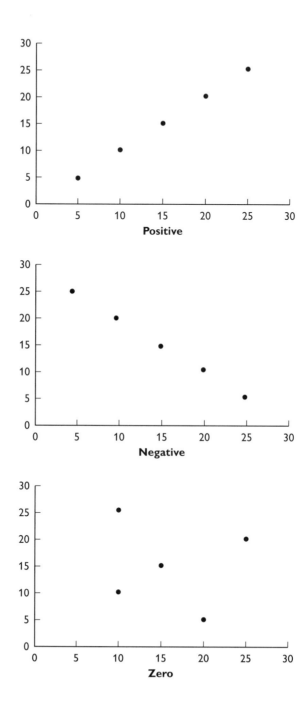

Figure 8 Scattergraphs to show positive, negative and zero correlations

Ethics

Specification content

An awareness of the code of ethics in psychology as specified by the British Psychological Society. The application of the code of ethics in psychological research.

Code of ethics specified by the British Psychological Society

The Code of Ethics and Conduct (2006), set out by the British Psychological Society (BPS), protects participants, patients and clients, maintains professional standards, provides a framework and guides decisions about appropriate conduct. The guidelines cover the professional and research activities of all psychologists. They apply to everyone carrying out psychological research, including students. You need to be aware of ethical issues relating to psychological research and follow the guidelines in any practical activities.

Applying the code of ethics in research

The code specifies four headings: respect, competence, responsibility, integrity.

- **Respect** — psychologists should respect individuals and avoid unfairness and prejudice. Information about people should be kept **confidential**. **Informed consent** must be sought, meaning that participants should know what they are consenting to. Parental consent is normally obtained for participants under 16 years old. **Privacy** should be respected in observations. **Deception** should be avoided wherever possible. If participants must be deceived, then they should be informed as soon as possible. Participants should have a **right to withdraw** either themselves or their data from research at any time.
- **Competence** — only qualified psychologists should give advice.
- **Responsibility** — participants must be **protected from harm**. Psychologists must **debrief** research participants after the investigation, telling them details of the research and its purpose.
- **Integrity** — psychologists should be honest and maintain professional boundaries.

An easy way to remember the key ethical issues in psychological research is to use the memory technique **CCDDPPW**:

- Consent
- Confidentiality
- Deception
- Debrief
- Protection
- Privacy
- Withdrawal

Questions
&
Answers

In this section of the guide there are six questions — two on Approaches, two on Gender Development and two on Research Methods. Each question is worth 20 marks. You should allow 30 minutes when answering each question. This section is structured as follows:

- sample question in the style in which they appear on the Unit 1 question paper
- analysis of the question, explaining what is expected in each sub-section of the question
- examples of candidate responses; these have been selected to illustrate particular strengths and limitations

Examiner comments

All candidate responses are followed by examiner comments, preceded by the icon ℮. Examiner comments explain how the marks have been awarded, aspects of the answer that are especially creditworthy and possible areas for improvement.

Approaches (I)

(a) What do humanistic psychologists mean by the term *conditions of worth*? Give an example of how a teacher might impose conditions of worth on her pupils. (2 marks)

(b) Marylou and Marianne are identical twins. When they were young, people could not tell them apart. Now that they are in their 50s, it is easy to tell them apart because Marylou is very slim with fine clear skin, whereas Marianne weighs a lot more and has skin that is heavily veined and lined.

With reference to both Marylou and Marianne, explain what is meant by the terms *genotype* and *phenotype*. (4 marks)

(c) Describe how cognitive psychologists use models to explain internal mental processes. (4 marks)

(d) Describe and evaluate the behaviourist approach in psychology. Refer to *one* other approach in your answer. (10 marks)

Total: 20 marks

(a) This is asking you to do two things and you would get a mark for each. First you need to state what is meant by the term. Second, you need to give an example relating to the question. Questions asking for an example will usually ask you to give an example in a specific context; in this case, the example is relating to a school situation.

(b) There are two distinct requirements. First you need to define the terms 'genotype' and 'phenotype'. Each correct definition is worth 1 mark. For the other 2 marks you need to link your definitions to the scenario taking care to refer to both the characters for full marks.

(c) This tests your knowledge of how science works and practical psychology by asking you about what cognitive psychologists do when they are studying mental processes. You need to explain what a model is, give an example of one and say what it shows about internal mental processes.

(d) Here you are expected to show your knowledge of the behaviourist approach by offering a clear description. Remember it is always important to use any specialist terminology — this shows you have been studying the topic. Half of the marks in these straightforward extended writing questions are for knowledge and description. The remaining marks are for evaluation, i.e. presenting strengths and limitations and using evidence to support what you say. In this question you are also invited to 'refer to one other approach' in your answer. This instruction is not meant to make the question any harder, but is meant to help you by suggesting that you compare the behaviourist approach with another approach as a way of obtaining more marks for evaluation and analysis. It is important to remember that if you fail to comply with any instruction asking you to 'refer to another…', or 'refer to evidence…', then you will gain a maximum of 6 marks however good the rest of the answer may be.

■ ■ ■

Answer to question 1: candidate A

(a) Humanistic psychologists say that conditions of worth are when a person does not feel loved and accepted. A teacher might do this by not accepting and valuing the pupils in her class who are naughty.

> Here the candidate almost defines conditions of worth, but does not quite capture the most essential part of the definition, i.e. that individuals will only be accepted and valued if they behave in ways that other people want them to. This idea is covered by the example so the candidate gets 1 mark out of 2.

(b) A genotype is the person's genes that they have. These are identical twins and so they have identical genes (100% the same), which means that they have identical genotypes. The phenotype is the final result and these twins look different by the time they reach the age of 50 years.

> The definition of a genotype is just about sufficient to gain a mark and the candidate correctly states that the twins have identical genotypes for a second mark. The definition of a phenotype is not explicit enough for further credit, and is not explained in the attempt to link back to the text. It does look as if the candidate knows what a phenotype is, but unfortunately he/she has not explained the issue of the interaction between genes and environment. In all, this answer is worth 2 out of the 4 marks.

(c) Cognitive psychologists use models of memory to explain internal mental processes. A model is a theory but is presented as a flowchart with arrows going from one section to another. In memory, for instance, there are three stages in the model: sensory memory, short-term memory and long-term memory. Once the cognitive psychologist has come up with the model, it means that other psychologists can use it to design their own studies of memory.

> The first sentence is entirely redundant because it simply repeats the question. In the second sentence the candidate shows understanding of what a model is in this context, and in the next sentence goes on to amplify this point in an example, the multi-store model of memory. The final sentence gives a basic but quite sound description of how the model is used. Although not always well expressed, this is actually a good answer and gets 3 marks out of 4. Various points might have been made to secure the extra mark, e.g. that internal mental processes cannot be seen and therefore need to be made more tangible; or that models are working hypotheses based on inference.

(d) The behaviourist approach includes classical and operant conditioning. Behaviourists believe that all behaviour is learnt and that we should not study anything that cannot be seen; for example, we should not study thinking processes and memory and so on as these are internal mental processes and so there have to be models used to explain them. Classical conditioning was devised by Pavlov who studied dog salivation and found that the dog would produce saliva to the sound of a bell because the bell was always presented at the same time as the food, which naturally would produce salivation. This study has been called unethical because the dog was tied up in a harness and had a tube fixed into its throat. However, it is better to do this kind of study with animals than to do it with people. This is one of the troubles with the behaviourist approach because they use animals and this is not useful to tell us about human behaviour and learning. They didn't really do any research with humans and so it is difficult to generalise. The behaviourist approach is no longer as popular as it was but it did gain a scientific reputation for psychology because of the methods being controlled and laboratory based.

The answer is not well organised; there are some inaccuracies and it sometimes goes off track. However, there is some useful description and evaluation of the approach. Notice how the candidate makes the fairly common mistake of using material from a previous sub-section on internal mental processes, apparently forgetting what this sub-section of the question is asking. He/she realises the mistake and soon gets back on track. Interestingly this detour into internal mental processes could have been used to good effect here by making a link between the behaviourist approach and the cognitive approach for more evaluation marks. As it is, the candidate has not mentioned another approach at all, and therefore could not get more than 6 marks overall.

The following three points were awarded marks for description: the basic principle that all behaviour is learnt; the idea that only outward behaviour should be the subject of psychological study and why; the knowledge of the basic procedure of classical conditioning, although this is not done well. The evaluation is scattered about the answer and some of it relates more to Pavlov's research than to the behaviourist approach itself. The point about ethics is not really of relevance for this question, so does not gain credit. Evaluation marks were awarded for the following two points: the problem of generalising from animal research and the enhancement of the scientific reputation of psychology. This answer gains a total of 5 marks out of 10. (AO1 = 3, AO2 = 2)

Total for this question: 11 out of 20 marks

Answer to question 1: candidate B

(a) The term 'conditions of worth' refers to the idea that people will only be valued by others if they behave in acceptable ways. The teacher might say to a child in her class that she will only want him in her class next year if he gets an A grade in his AS examination.

✅ Here the candidate defines the term clearly and gives a good example. This answer is worth the full 2 marks.

(b) A genotype is a person's genetic make-up. Identical or MZ twins are from the same fertilised egg and therefore have an identical genetic make-up, so Marylou and Marianne share 100% of their genes in common and have the same genotype. A phenotype is the expression of the genotype in the individual and is the result of the interaction between the genotype and the environment. Marylou and Marianne have different phenotypes, which is why they look different even though they have the same genotype.

✅ Both terms are defined clearly using correct terminology and both are linked precisely to the cases of Marylou and Marianne. This answer deserves the full 4 marks.

(c) Internal mental processes like memory cannot be directly observed; therefore cognitive psychology proposes models which are really hypotheses about the structure and organisation of thinking processes. One example is the multi-store model of memory proposed by Atkinson and Shiffrin in 1968. This is a theory about how memory is organised. The model provides a framework for further investigation, stimulating research by other memory researchers.

✅ The first sentence almost provides a complete full-mark answer in itself. This candidate starts by noting the essential problem with studying internal processes: that they cannot be directly observed. Next, he/she notes how a model is a way of helping us to understand the process we cannot see. Another further relevant point, that models indicate the ways in which a process is structured or organised, is also worth credit. Further creditworthy content includes the example and what it shows, with an added note about the model's usefulness for further research. The full 4 marks are awarded here.

(d) The behaviourist approach became popular in the US where psychologists like Pavlov and Skinner carried out controlled scientific experiments about learning using animals. All behaviourist research takes place in controlled conditions so that variables can be isolated and cause and effect can be determined. Behaviourists believe that all behaviour is learnt and behaviour depends on consequences. In a typical operant conditioning study, Skinner showed how learning bar-pressing behaviour in rats depended on whether or not the rat received a food pellet as reinforcement. Rats would rapidly learn that the action of bar-pressing resulted in a pleasant consequence, so they would repeat the action. Skinner called this positive reinforcement.

Behaviourists also assume that only external behaviour is valid subject matter for psychologists, if psychology is to be scientific. As such they restricted their observations to outward behaviour and did not study emotions and thoughts which some people like Freud would consider of great importance. In this way there is

a great difference between the behaviourists and the psychodynamic psychologists like Freud, whose study of the unconscious would have been strongly criticised by behaviourists for being totally unscientific.

The behaviourists can be credited with making psychology respectable as a
science but have been criticised for neglecting the importance of mental life. In
choosing to study animal behaviour in highly controlled artificial conditions, their
research could be said to have little validity in relation to everyday human behaviour. The behaviourists have also been criticised for taking a mechanical view of
human beings, assuming that people are responding machines that can be
controlled by reinforcement, and that we have no free will.

This is a thorough answer that meets the requirement to refer to another
approach quite effectively. Notice how the reference to the psychodynamic
approach enables a useful contrast and is used by the candidate to make an
evaluative point about the importance of studying thoughts and emotions as well
as behaviour. There are several creditworthy descriptive points in the first
paragraph and at the start of the second: the reference to controlled research; the
idea that all behaviour is learnt and that learning depends on consequences; the
description of operant conditioning with correct use of terminology; the
importance of studying only external behaviour.

As already noted, the comparison with Freud gains credit as evaluation/analysis and
there are several other evaluative points to credit: the reference to scientific
respectability; the use of animal research; the artificiality of controlled environ-
ments; the mechanistic view.

Taken as a whole, this answer provides an interesting description that covers most
of the assumptions of the behaviourist approach and includes some well-argued
evaluation and analysis. The slight inaccuracy of placing Pavlov in the USA is incon-
sequential to the content and therefore does not affect the credit awarded. The
answer gains 10 marks out of 10. (AO1 = 5, AO2 = 5)

Total for this question: 20 out of 20 marks

Approaches (II)

(a) Sally often watches her mother brushing her hair and putting on her make-up. According to social learning theory, Sally might imitate her mother's actions but this would depend on mediating cognitive factors.

State what social learning theorists mean by *mediating cognitive factors*, and suggest *two* ways in which mediating factors might affect Sally's behaviour in this situation. (3 marks)

(b) Identify and outline *one* defence mechanism and suggest how it might help a person to cope with failing a driving test. (3 marks)

(c) Outline two methods that have been used to study cortical specialisation. (4 marks)

(d) Describe and evaluate the biological approach in psychology. Refer to evidence in your answer. (10 marks)

Total: 20 marks

(a) This is an application question where you are required to show your under-standing by applying what you know, in this case about social learning theory, to a novel situation. Notice the two parts to the question; first you need to define the term for 1 mark; second you need to make two clear links with the scenario for the other 2 marks.

(b) There is a mark for naming a defence mechanism, for example, repression; and another mark for outlining what it means, for example, you might say that repression is motivated forgetting. The third mark is for explaining how the defence mechanism might be used by a person who has failed his/her driving test. You then need to make a link between the defence mechanism you have chosen and the scenario. A common error in this sort of question is to identify one defence mechanism and then explain a different one. Think before you write the name of the first defence mechanism you can think of. Do you really know what it is and can you link it effectively to the scenario?

(c) This is straightforward. The instruction to outline simply means that you should give a brief description. An extremely brief or slightly inaccurate outline would be worth 1 mark, with 2 marks for an accurate outline that includes correct terminology. If you outline more than two methods the examiner would credit the two best outlines, but you would have wasted precious time. It is much better to think first which two would enable you to offer the most detailed outline.

(d) Half of the marks are for description and the other half of the marks are for evaluation and analysis. Here you are asked to demonstrate knowledge of the biological approach by offering a clear description, which is probably best done by considering the basic assumptions. Particularly in this area it is important to use the correct terminology to show that you have been studying the topic.

The marks for evaluation can be gained by presenting strengths and limitations and using evidence to support what you say. In this question you are asked to 'refer to evidence' in your answer. Remember that if you fail to comply with this instruction, you will be limited to a maximum of 6 marks.

■ ■ ■

Answer to question 2: candidate A

(a) 'Mediating cognitive' factors is a term used to refer to the thinking that comes between the stimulus and the response. In this case, Sally would have to pay attention to what her mum does and also remember how to do it so she can copy her.

🖉 This is a full-mark answer. There is a definition and then two good examples of cognitive mediators: paying attention and remembering.

(b) One defence mechanism is displacement. Displacement is where you project your feelings onto something else. In this case, you could slam the door when you get out of the car instead of screaming at the examiner. This would make you feel much better, which is what defence mechanisms do.

🖉 Here the candidate names an appropriate defence mechanism so gets 1 mark, but the definition is not that clear, mainly because of the use of the word 'project' which is not the right word here. In fact, projection is a different defence mechanism altogether. You should note that displacement and projection are often confused by candidates in exams. The example is a good one and relevant to the situation, so the candidate gets 2 out of 3 marks for part (b).

(c) The first method is using scans. A scan is where a machine (PET or MRI) is used to show the parts of the brain that are active when a person is carrying out different activities. Quite often the person is injected with a substance of radioactive properties, which then lights up in a different colour on the scan when that bit of the brain is engaged in a task.

The second method is surgery on the brain. This would only happen with a person who is ill and would not happen for experimental purposes. Perhaps a part of the brain would be cut out, for example to prevent epileptic fits as with HM. We could then see if other abilities were affected. In HM's case he could not make any new memories.

🖉 The candidate correctly outlines scanning techniques. It does not matter that there is no clear distinction between different types of scans and there is enough detail and use of correct terminology here to merit 2 marks for this method. The second method is also sufficiently detailed to be awarded the full 2 marks; there is a description of the possible circumstances and the final sentences explain exactly how this method is used and offer an example. Although this would have been a full mark answer without the example, it is sometimes useful to provide one if you do not feel you have explained something well. The example might just help to clarify and might persuade the examiner that you do know what you are talking about.

question

(d) The biological approach is one of the most scientific approaches used by psychologists studying behaviour. This is a big strength because it is always important to carry out controlled research and it also makes psychology more respectable as a science.

One topic of interest for biopsychologists is the study of brain structure, for example showing which parts of the brain are responsible for different abilities and functions. For example, Hubel and Wiesel looked at cells in the visual area of the brain and found that particular cells were specialised for different visual functions. Discoveries like this help psychologists to treat people who have problems and biological therapies are often used.

Biopsychologists are also involved in studying brain chemicals and hormones. Some interesting hormones are the sex hormones, oestrogen and testosterone. Finding out about how these affect our behaviour is useful to help treat illnesses.

A problem with the biological approach in psychology is that a lot of the research is carried out using animals. As an example, cutting out the hypothalamus in a rat means that it can no longer learn and memorise locations or a route. The findings are then used to try to explain human behaviour. Many people would argue that humans are more complex creatures than other animals and that it is therefore quite wrong to generalise. On the other hand, biological psychologists might feel it is justified because, as Darwin stated, all species are related so we probably have some functions and processes in common with other animals.

This answer starts well with a clear statement about the scientific status of the biological approach. The first paragraph is awarded 1 description mark for the point about science and control and an evaluation mark for explaining how this has affected the status of psychology. In the second paragraph there is a useful description of the study of brain structure and function for another description mark. This is backed up with reference to Hubel and Wiesel's research, which is described sufficiently for another mark. The final evaluative point is a little bit general but is nevertheless worth a mark. The third paragraph is awarded another mark for knowledge of another aspect of the biological approach, but the evaluative point at the end is brief and, in any case, merely a repeat of a previous point. In the final paragraph there is an example of animal research and an extended discussion of the use of animals in psychological research and the issue of generalisation. There is a nice balance here with arguments for and against which works well. In all, this paragraph is awarded another description mark and 2 evaluation marks. As a whole, the answer covers several issues, includes relevant evidence and shows some quite mature and developed evaluation. In total 9 marks are awarded. (AO1 = 5, AO2 = 4)

Total for this question: 18 out of 20 marks

Answer to question 2: candidate B

(a) These are cognitive factors that mediate between seeing and copying, so in Sally's case she is watching and mentally noting and is therefore able to do the same.

> 🖉 The candidate attempts to define the term but uses the same terms and therefore cannot get the mark for the definition. As far as the application goes, 1 mark is awarded for 'mentally noting' which is a reference to memory. The reference to 'watching' is behavioural rather than cognitive, so does not get the second mark for application. Perhaps the candidate means to refer to attention here but it is not clear. Only 1 mark is awarded for this section.

(b) Freud said defence mechanisms help us deal with unpleasant events. There are several defence mechanisms. Rationalisation is a useful one. It helps you to be rational, although if you are upset it is hard to be rational. Here the driver might think that there are already too many cars on the road, so it is really a good thing that he has failed.

> 🖉 This answer starts with a definition of defence mechanisms in general, which is not required. A mark is awarded for rationalisation, although the definition is uninformative and even uses the same term. The example is plausible, however, and is therefore awarded a mark. In all, this part of the answer gets 2 out of 3 marks.

(c) Several methods are useful. One common method is the use of psychosurgery. In some studies people have the two halves of their brain completely severed. They then find it difficult to see properly with two eyes at the same time. It can, however, be useful to control the effects of mental disorders. Another method is the use of an ECG. This is where electrodes are attached to the scalp and the activity can be seen on a screen.

> 🖉 This candidate offers enough of an outline of neurosurgery for 1 mark. He/she seems to be describing split-brain studies although there is a lack of accuracy. The second method at first appears as if it will not attract any marks because there is confusion between EEG (use of electrodes to record brain activity) and ECG (use of electrodes to record heart activity). The final sentence has helped the candidate to achieve 1 mark because there is reference to the scalp, indicating that he/she is discussing brain activity rather than heart activity, so 2 marks are awarded here.

(d) The biological approach is about the study of genes and physical factors that affect behaviour. Twin studies show that lots of behaviours and abilities are related to genetics, and that we inherit them from our parents. Things like intelligence and mental illness etc. could all be genetic in the code of DNA. This code exists in every cell in the body. If twins are found to be alike in one area, then we will assume that whatever it is, for example mental illness, is probably genetic. There are two types of twins. Identical twins have all the same genes because they come from a single egg. Non-identical twins are not all the same genetically because they come from two different eggs. One piece of evidence for this is the study by Bouchard on intelligence in twins. It was found that identical twins had similar intelligence test scores, more similar than non-identical twins. This is support for the biological approach to intelligence.

question

People criticise the biological approach for being too oversimplified. It ignores social influences on behaviour, for example people may become more intelligent because of the way they are treated rather than because of the genes they inherit, but the biological approach does not consider this. Another problem is that it might not be kind to treat people as if they are just biological machines. Biopsychologists use drugs, which is really interfering with nature.

The first paragraph is awarded 2 description marks; one for the general point about the focus on genetics and inheritance, and the other for reference to a piece of research. There is a rather protracted description of twins and twin studies which is a bit garbled and adds little. In fact, it rather takes the focus of the answer away from the biological approach in general. The end of the first paragraph is worthy of an evaluation mark for use of evidence. Several evaluative issues are noted in the second paragraph, although many are not developed sufficiently for credit. A mark is awarded for the point about ignoring social factors, and another, perhaps rather generously, for the last two sentences where the candidate touches briefly on ethical issues and treatments. Overall the answer lacks information. There is fairly minimal description of the approach and some of the evaluative points need further explanation. This section of the answer gets 5 marks. (AO1 = 2, AO2 = 3)

Total for this question: 10 out of 20 marks

Gender development (I)

(a) (i) Outline what psychologists mean by *androgyny*. (2 marks)

   (ii) Describe *one* way in which psychologists have studied androgyny. (2 marks)

(b) Identify and explain *one* limitation of the psychodynamic approach to explaining gender development. (3 marks)

(c) Suggest how a developmental psychologist might investigate gender stability in a child aged 5 years. (3 marks)

(d) Discuss nature and nurture in relation to gender development. (10 marks)

Total: 20 marks

   (a) (i) This is asking for a clear definition. For 2 marks you are expected to provide some elaboration or detail, e.g. use of additional terminology such as 'masculine' and 'feminine' would be good elaboration here.

   (ii) This assesses your knowledge of research into androgyny. Note that this is not a full 'Describe a study' question because it is only worth 2 marks. In this question, the focus is simply on the method and not on any one particular study. The most likely answer here will be based on the Bem sex-role inventory. Since there is a lot you could say, it should be relatively easy to give enough detail for 2 marks.

   (b) Here you will get 1 mark for identifying a valid limitation. The instruction to 'explain' requires you to elaborate on how or why it is a limitation. When you see the word 'explain' in any question, you should always try to think 'how?' or 'why?' In this question, it is important to remember that you need to think of a limitation that relates to the explanation of gender development and not any old limitation of the psychodynamic approach.

   (c) This assesses your understanding of how psychologists carry out research. You need to think what the term 'gender stability' means and then you should be able to recall how gender stability was studied. The wording of the question does allow for any feasible method; so if you can't recall any research into gender stability, but do know what it means, you could propose your own way of studying gender stability. Whether or not this would gain any marks depends on whether what you propose has any face validity. In other words, does the method appear to measure what it is supposed to measure? For the full 3 marks the method must be plausible, must relate to gender stability and must be appropriate for a 5-year-old child.

   (d) The best way to approach this is to first outline the terms 'nature' and 'nurture', showing that you understand something about the debate. Thereafter this would become a two-sided answer; on the one hand you should present theory and evidence to support the nature side of the argument (the biological explanation for gender and associated research); you should then balance the answer by offering theory and evidence relating to the nurture side of the debate (the social learning explanation for gender and associated research). In this question the AO2 marks for evaluation and analysis are likely to come from appropriate use of evidence, linking it to the key issues in the question, and for comparison of the two sides of the debate. If there is time, you could also include any nature–nurture aspects of psychodynamic and cognitive theories. As with most debates in psychology, offering a balanced, inter-actionist view as a conclusion would be a sensible way to finish this answer.

■ ■ ■

Answer to question 3: candidate A

(a) (i) Androgyny means behaving like a man and a woman at the same time, where someone is showing attitudes and abilities of each gender.

> This answer gets 2 marks. It is not a well-expressed response but the candidate has the general idea, focusing not just on immediate behaviour but also on more enduring traits.

(ii) Bem studied androgyny using a questionnaire. People had to say which characteristics they were like, and then they got a score for being male and a score for being female at the end. Together this was their androgyny score.

> This is a basic answer mentioning the questionnaire briefly and the idea that respondents get two scores at the end. There is a lack of detail and some poor expression, but the answer nevertheless conveys the key information about Bem's questionnaire yielding two separate scores. This answer is awarded a rather generous 2 marks out of 2.

(b) One problem with the psychodynamic approach to explaining gender is that Freud had no evidence for what he proposed like the Oedipus complex.

> The candidate identifies a valid limitation for 1 mark but there is no further explanation. It is worth noting how the answer is just about related to the development of gender through the reference to the Oedipus complex. Without that there would have been no clear link to gender and the answer would not have gained any marks. There is some opportunity for further marks here. For example, the candidate could have explained how the Oedipus complex involves an unconscious conflict and that is why it does not lend itself to scientific study.

(c) Gender stability can be studied by asking a child about when they were little. If a child has gender stability they will answer correctly and know that they were always male or female.

> The method described here is vague but could just about be seen as a valid way of measuring gender identity, and understanding of the term is implicit. Because the answer is so vague, only 1 mark is given here.

(d) Over the years many psychologists have said that gender is due to biology. Males and females have different sex chromosomes so it is these that are responsible for gender. In other words, girls are gentle and passive because they do not have a Y chromosome and therefore no testosterone. Males, on the other hand, are aggressive and competitive because they do possess the male Y chromosome and so have testosterone. Injecting animals with testosterone does increase aggression.

Other psychologists believe that gender is learnt and can be affected by how we are treated. The theory of neutrality (Money) stated that babies in the womb are not either male or female, but will turn out either way because of how they are treated when they are born. To test this, a young boy who had lost his penis in a dreadful accident was brought up as a girl. He was socialised altogether as a girl, given girls' toys to play with, dressed as a girl and also had surgery to make him into a female. However, this study did not end up as the researchers expected because when he reached puberty he decided he did not want to carry on with the treatment and so became a boy again in his behaviour and attitudes. There are many ethical problems with this study. The researchers have been accused of using the boy to test their theory and the consequences were unhappy for him and his family.

Going back to the debate, there is evidence that both nature and nurture are involved in gender, probably in equal measures.

The answer starts without any explicit reference to nature and nurture which is meant to be the focus of the question. Indeed, these terms do not appear at all until the concluding sentence. It is left to the examiner to make links between the content and the question because none are provided by the candidate. This is not a good strategy because examiners should not have to make the effort for you, and may not give you the benefit of the doubt. Remember to always keep your points focused directly on the question. That said, the first paragraph is awarded 2 marks for knowledge of the biological side (nature) of the debate. The final sentence about injecting animals with testosterone was not awarded any marks because there is no obvious link to the question. It could have been made relevant by explaining how such evidence supports the nature side of the debate.

At the start of the second paragraph the candidate gets a mark for outlining the opposite view, that gender might be learnt, although once again, there is no explicit reference to the debate. The description of the Money study is long-winded and adds little to the answer; however, 1 mark is awarded for a description of a valid study. Had the candidate explained how the study might be linked to nature or nurture, then more marks would have been awarded. The ethical evaluation of the Money study at the end of the paragraph is wholly irrelevant to this question. The final mention of nature–nurture at the end of the answer is not really sufficient to be awarded any further marks. In all, this sub-section answer is awarded 4 marks out of 10. Notice that this candidate has not been awarded any of the five AO2 marks available for evaluation or discussion. This could have been addressed quite easily, using little extra material, simply by explaining how the content offered here links to either nature or nurture (AO1 = 4, AO2 = 0)

Total for this question: 10 out of 20 marks

Answer to question 3: candidate B

(a) (i) Androgyny refers to a person showing a balanced combination of typically masculine and typically feminine traits and characteristics.

This answer gets full marks. The candidate expresses the meaning clearly using appropriate terminology — for example, the terms masculine and feminine.

(ii) Sandra Bem invented the Bem sex-role inventory (BSRI). Respondents have to rate themselves on a scale for 60 adjectives, e.g. shy, forceful etc. Some of the adjectives are typically male and some are typically female. The person's overall masculinity score and femininity score can be calculated at the end, showing whether he/she is androgynous or not.

This is an excellent full-mark answer. It is clearly expressed and includes ample detail of how androgyny has been studied.

(b) According to Freud gender arises in the phallic stage when the child is approximately 4 or 5 years old. This would mean that a child younger than 4 years should not really show any awareness of gender or gender-typed behaviours. However, cognitive psychologists like Kohlberg have shown that children show understanding of gender before the age of 4 years when they have gender identity. These findings suggest that Freud's theory was incorrect.

Here the candidate offers a valid limitation of the psychodynamic approach which is clearly linked to gender. This shows sound understanding, is well expressed, and includes a full and logical explanation of the problem. This answer is easily worth the full 3 marks.

(c) Gender stability comes after gender identity. It is the ability to realise that gender is constant and that we will always be the same gender, and have always been the same in the past. Children get to understand this when about 4 years old, according to Slaby and Frey, who asked children questions like 'When you were a baby, were you a baby girl or a baby boy?' and 'When you grow up will you be a mummy or a daddy?' Depending on the answer, you can tell if they know their gender is the same at all times. For example, if a boy said he used to be a baby girl then he would not show gender stability.

This is a full-mark answer. The answer starts with a definition which shows that the candidate has a good understanding of what is meant by gender stability. A suitable method is described clearly, the reasoning is sound and the answer is finished off nicely with a sentence explaining how the responses to the questions would relate to gender stability.

(d) Psychologists take different views on the debate about the relative influence of nature and nurture on gender. The extreme nature side would argue that gender is entirely biological, and the extreme nurture side would suggest that gender is entirely due to socialisation as male or female. In reality, it is most likely that both nature and nurture contribute to gender development.

Supporting the nature argument, psychologists have found that biological differences between males and females affect not only physical characteristics, but also gender-related behaviour. For example, body builders taking male hormones show higher than normal aggression scores on questionnaires. Animal studies, too, support the view that biology (nature) affects gender-related behaviour, although it is difficult to generalise from animal research to humans. There are similar problems with case study research, e.g. Money's case of Bruce. Such unusual cases seem to show that biology can overrule socialisation, but both are so unusual that they are not that useful to explain normal gender development. It would seem that those who strongly favour the nature side totally disregard the influence of parents and the environment on gender.

This contrasts with the nurture view, which suggests that males and females behave differently because they are reinforced for different types of behaviour. For example, girls are reinforced for behaving gently whilst boys are reinforced for being rough. Studies such as Baby X and Fagot showed that adults and parents do treat male and female infants differently, so supporting the nurture argument. Social learning theory states that people will observe and imitate the behaviour of models; for a young boy the model with whom he closely identifies would be the father, and for a girl, the mother. SLT would therefore support the nurture side of the debate, showing that even if there was no reinforcement, children would inevitably copy the behaviour of a same-sex model.

Cross-cultural studies also explore the influence of nurture. If there are differences in gender behaviour in different cultures, this would suggest that gender is influenced more by nurture, i.e. upbringing and environment, than by biology. Mead's study showed that there are cultural differences, and although she was criticised for being subjective, the same has been found elsewhere.

To conclude the argument, it is inevitable that gender is determined both by nature, in the form of X and Y chromosomes, hormones and brain structure, and by nurture, in the form of social learning through observation and reinforcement. In either case, it seems that gender is determined by internal or external factors and so we do not have free will to choose to behave as either masculine or feminine.

🖉 Notice how this candidate starts by explicitly defining the terms nature and nurture, and then relates them directly to the issue of gender. Having done this at the start, it then makes it much easier for the examiner to see what follows in the context of nature and nurture, and therefore makes it much easier for the candidate to get marks. In the second paragraph, the candidate offers evidence for the nature side of the argument and clearly relates this to the question by using phrases like 'supporting the nature argument' and 'supports the view'. In this way he/she gains AO1 marks for description and knowledge, but also gains AO2 evaluation and analysis marks for the use of evidence. At the end of the nature paragraph, the candidate gains a further evaluation mark for making a contrasting reference relating to the role of parents and environment which then leads into the next paragraph. In the discussion of social learning and reinforcement, the

question

candidate makes frequent references back to the issue of nurture and links psychological evidence and theory directly to the question about nurture and gender. Here again, AO1 marks are awarded for knowledge and AO2 marks for use of that knowledge and evidence to answer the question. The final concluding paragraph brings together the whole with a neat summary of the interactionist perspective and makes a highly perceptive comment about how both nature and nurture see gender as somehow determined. There is ample content for full marks here. The answer focuses on the question, offers a balance of evidence for each side and links every point sensibly to the question of nature and nurture. (AO1 = 5, AO2 = 5)

Total for this question: 20 out of 20 marks

Gender development (II)

(a) (i) Identify *one* androgen. (1 mark)

(ii) Briefly describe *one* method used by psychologists to investigate the influence of androgens on behaviour. (2 marks)

(b) James is hoping to train as a nurse when he leaves school but his father is trying to persuade him not to. 'Why don't you look at engineering?' says his father hopefully, 'That would be a much better option.'

Explain what is meant by *sex-role stereotyping*. Refer to James in your answer. (3 marks)

(c) Outline and briefly evaluate *one* study that supports the social learning explanation for gender development. (4 marks)

(d) Describe and evaluate *two* cognitive approaches to explaining gender. (10 marks)

Total: 20 marks

(a) (i) Here you are required to simply state the name of an androgen (male hormone). There is no need to write a sentence, a single word answer will suffice.

(ii) This asks for a brief description. Generally speaking, if 2 marks are on offer then you should try to make two points. Here, for example, 1 mark will be for briefly noting an appropriate method, for example looking at groups with naturally occurring high levels of male hormone, e.g. people with CAH. The second mark will be for describing how this method can be used to tell us anything about the origin of gender-related behaviour.

(b) Here, 2 of the marks are for defining the term. A good definition would include some mention of 'accepted attitudes/behaviour' or 'expected attitudes/behaviour' and then a reference to males and females. The third mark is for linking the definition to something in the text, for example by commenting on James's father's expectations of his son.

(c) This has two distinct elements. To provide a 2-mark outline you need to offer a brief description of a relevant study by noting the method and the findings. The 2-mark discussion part of the question requires you to make some evaluation. You may choose one point and elaborate on it in a couple of sentences, or make two separate points briefly.

(d) Here is a straightforward question with 5 AO1 marks for knowledge of two cognitive approaches (Kohlberg and gender schema theory would be the ones to use) and 5 AO2 marks for evaluation, discussion and comparison. It is important to realise that you must offer two cognitive approaches. If you only cover one, then the maximum marks available would be 6 out of 10. Although the question does not ask for evidence, in 10-mark questions at least 1 mark may be awarded for knowledge of a relevant study, for example Slaby and Frey's gender concept interview or Damon's study of the boy George. Using evidence also allows you to gain AO2 marks by

question

explaining how the evidence supports the theory, or otherwise. Your answer can be structured in two ways. You could cover the two approaches sequentially, describing one approach and evaluating it, then describing the other approach and evaluating it. This is probably the route that most students would prefer. Alternatively, you could integrate descriptions of both the approaches, comparing them and evaluating them as you mention the different aspects. Whichever way you choose to answer, it is possible to access the full 10 marks.

■ ■ ■

Answer to question 4: candidate A

(a) (i) Testosterone is an androgen.

🖉 This gets 1 mark.

(ii) One method is to use female animals. They can be injected with male hormone to see whether it alters their behaviour to be more like that of a male.

🖉 This is worth the full 2 marks. There is a clear description and an indication of how the outcome would relate to gender-related behaviour.

(b) Sex-role stereotyping is where all members of a particular sex are assumed or expected to be the same. For example, all males are expected to be tough and all females are expected to be gentle. James's father shows sex-role stereotyping by expecting him to be something traditionally male like an engineer.

🖉 The first sentence offers a reasonable definition which is further clarified by the examples. If an examiner is in any doubt about whether to award a mark or not, it is sometimes useful if the candidate does offer an example. This might help the examiner to decide between 1 mark or 2 marks. In this case, 2 marks are awarded for the definition and 1 mark for the sensible link to the text.

(c) Fagot observed toddlers interacting with parents in their homes. It was found that boys and girls were reinforced and encouraged for different sorts of behaviours. A good thing about this was that it had high ecological validity and so was not artificial.

🖉 This answer clearly notes the method and findings of a relevant study. The point about high ecological validity is sensible and just about sufficiently explained for 1 mark. This issue could have been explored in a little more depth if the candidate had noted how behaviour studied in a natural context is more like normal, everyday behaviour. In all, this answer gets 2 marks for the outline and 1 mark for the evaluation.

(d) One cognitive approach to gender is Kohlberg's theory. He focused on how a child understands gender and thought that gender understanding gets more complex with age and occurs in three stages. The first stage is the gender identity stage where a child around 2 years of age understands what sex he/she is and what sex other people are. The next stage is the gender stability stage where children about 4 years old understand that their gender stays the same in the future. In the final stage of gender constancy, the child of 7 years plus understands that gender stays the same even if outside appearance like clothes or context changes.

Kohlberg's theory describes well and in detail what happens but it doesn't really explain why the child's understanding changes over time. There is evidence to support Kohlberg's theory though. In interviews Slaby and Frey showed that the stages exist when they asked questions to investigate the different stages. For example, a child of 3 years old might not understand that he will remain for ever a boy even though he knows that he is a boy at the moment.

Gender schema theory was proposed by Martin and Halverson. They state that once children realise what they are, male or female, they start to focus on things associated with their own sex and avoid things from the other sex. In this way they build up a schema of 'boy' or 'girl'. This schema then affects how they behave as males or females because the schema is used to guide future behaviour. For example, if a boy knows boys like cars then he will spend more time playing with cars than dolls. Gender schema theory is an improvement on Kohlberg's theory because it explains gender behaviour and not just understanding. It is also a step up from social learning theory because it shows why children imitate models selectively because it fits with their gender schema of what is appropriate for their sex. Despite their great successes, cognitive theories of gender cannot explain gender development on their own. There is probably some biological influence to gender as well.

This is a good answer, even though there is possibly greater focus on Kohlberg's theory than on gender schema theory. There is a clear description of Kohlberg's theory showing knowledge and understanding of all three stages, which are named correctly, and expressing clearly the basic idea that gender understanding becomes more sophisticated with age. The description of gender schema theory is less detailed but nevertheless accurate and nicely clarified with the use of an example. Although the question does not ask for evidence it is provided here, and would get at least one AO1 mark, although in this case the candidate has done enough elsewhere to achieve the full 5 marks for description. There are a number of relevant evaluative points which gain AO2 marks. One of these marks is for use of evidence where the candidate links the findings of the study to the theory, and a further mark for evaluation comes from the analytical point about the limitation of Kohlberg's theory. The evaluation of gender schema theory includes comparison between the cognitive theories and also comparison with an alternative, namely social learning theory. The final point about cognitive theories in general is also creditworthy. This is a full-mark answer. (AO1 = 5, AO2 = 5)

Total for this question: 19 out of 20 marks

Answer to question 4: candidate B

(a) (i) Testosterone.

> 📝 This gets 1 mark.

(ii) One way is to use a correlation method. You could measure the amount or level of testosterone in a person's body and then get a measure of how masculine they are in their behaviour. You would expect a positive correlation if testosterone is linked to masculinity, with high masculinity being linked to high testosterone and vice versa.

> 📝 This is awarded full marks. There is a slight problem with the variable of masculinity because there is no clear idea of how this would be measured, but, given that this question is only worth 2 marks, the candidate has probably done enough here. The method is plausible and it is a good answer in the time available.

(b) A sex-role stereotype is where someone should be in a certain role for their sex and so they are being stereotyped. James does not want to be in the stereotype of a male profession because he is keen on a more female-oriented profession. His father is trying to stereotype him into being male. His father has no right to do this.

> 📝 This candidate does not really define the term. Notice how the first sentence, which is meant to be the definition, simply rearranges the words and does not offer anything more. The link to the text does get a mark however. Only 1 mark is awarded for this section.

(c) The Bandura Bobo doll study showed how children will copy behaviour. In this famous study, children saw an adult behaving aggressively with a doll. Later on, the children copied the model's aggression. This happened more if the model was a boy and the child was also a boy. One problem with this study is that it happened a long time ago. Another problem is the ethics of exposing children to aggression.

> 📝 This is a valid study as long as the candidate focuses on the gender aspect. You probably realise that there were many variations of this study carried out in the 1960s, each with a slightly different aim and method. Here, 1 mark is awarded for the outline because there is a brief reference to gender. There are two brief evaluative points given here. The first is not really explained at all. The candidate needs to say why it matters that the study took place a long time ago to get any credit. 1 mark is given for the ethical point. Had the candidate explained how it is important that participants in research are not exposed to harm, then the second mark could have been given. As it is, this answer gets a total of 2 marks out of 4 marks.

(d) One cognitive theory of gender is gender schema theory, which states that boys and girls develop a gender schema of what boys are and what girls are. In the stage theory it is stated that children develop a gender schema for their own gender first and then the other gender later. Another theory is Kohlberg's. His is also a stage theory but he doesn't say anything about understanding own gender first and other gender afterwards, although, of course, that could be the case. According to Kohlberg we can label ourselves first and can point to a photo of a boy or girl when asked. This is labelling. Later on we know that our gender has consistency and will be the same no matter what. The other stage is the stability stage where ideas remain stable for ever.

Alternatives to cognitive theory are the biological and social learning theory. Biologists assume that gender is all down to genes and chromosomes, and social learning theory believes that gender is learnt by watching other people like models and copying them. This was demonstrated in the Bobo doll study by Bandura.

🗩 The candidate makes one creditworthy point about gender schema theory with the reference to development of own-sex schema before other-sex schema. The general point about what a gender schema contains is also worth credit. The description of Kohlberg is rather confused and inaccurate, but perhaps worthy of a rather generous AO1 mark overall. There is a half-hearted comparison between gender schema theory and Kohlberg that is just about worth AO2 credit. The alternative theories are simply tagged on at the end without any attempt to compare them with cognitive theories. As such, this last paragraph is completely redundant and gets no credit at all. Always be careful when you present alternative theories as part of a discussion. These will only count if you make clear links between them and the theory under discussion. Stand alone alternatives, like the ones here, are worth nothing because they are not being used to answer the question. In all this answer gets 4 marks out of 10. (AO1 = 3, AO2 = 1)

Total for this question: 10 out of 20 marks

Research methods (I)

A biopsychologist investigating reaction time to different stimuli decides to carry out an experiment with two conditions. He recruits participants from the college canteen, asking anyone who is around to take part. He tells them that it is a 'fun experiment' and that he will explain it all to them afterwards.

In one condition, participants have to press a button on a computer as soon as they hear a noise through headphones they are wearing. In the other condition, the same participants, again wearing headphones, have to press the button as soon as they see a coloured light appear in the centre of the computer screen. Half of the participants perform in the light condition first and the noise condition second. For the other half of the participants the conditions are in the opposite order.

For each condition, the psychologist records the individual response times on five separate trials, and then takes the average response time for each participant. These averages are then used to calculate an overall average response time for each condition.

At the end of the study, when the psychologist debriefs the participants, one of them is upset when told that his reaction time of 200 milliseconds in the light condition is much higher than that of all the other participants.

Mean response time (in milliseconds) for the noise stimulus condition and the light stimulus condition

	Noise stimulus condition	Light stimulus condition
Mean response time (milliseconds)	80	60

(a) Sketch a bar graph that could be used to display the mean response times. Label and title your graph. (3 marks)

(b) The researcher uses the mean time in milliseconds as a measure of central tendency. Explain *one* problem of using the mean in this study. (2 marks)

(c) Name the experimental design the researcher used in this experiment. (1 mark)

(d) Explain why it was necessary for the order of conditions to be reversed for half of the participants. What is the name of this technique? (3 marks)

(e) Explain why it was important for the participants to wear the headphones in both conditions of the experiment. (2 marks)

(f) Explain *one* ethical problem involved in this study and suggest how it might have been avoided. (3 marks)

(g) The researcher decided to carry out an unstructured interview with the participant who had a very high reaction time in the light condition.

  (i) Explain what is meant by an *unstructured interview*. (2 marks)

  (ii) Suggest one reason why an unstructured interview might be useful in this situation. (1 mark)

(h) **The researcher obtained participants from the college canteen.**

    (i) **Identify the sampling technique used in this investigation.** (1 mark)

    (ii) **Suggest *one* strength and *one* limitation of this sampling technique.** (2 marks)

Total: 20 marks

(a) This asks for a sketch. There will probably be a section of graph paper in your answer book. Out of the 3 marks, 1 mark is for a title which should include the units of measurement (e.g. milliseconds) and the names of both conditions, 1 mark is for axis labels on the x- and y-axes, and the third mark is for plotting the graph.

(b) You are asked to link your answer to this study. This wording is often used in the research methods questions and means that you cannot offer any old problem (in this case with the use of the mean), but must gear your answer specifically to the study described.

(c) Here you are simply asked to name the experimental design so there is no need to write a sentence if you know the name. If you don't know the exact name for the design, but could try to describe it, then you might get a mark for that. It is worth a go.

(d) This requires a named technique associated with the experimental design used for the study. As in the previous question, it is worth describing the technique if you don't know the name for it as you might get a mark. The other 2 marks are for explaining why the technique was used. Again, it would be sensible to link your answer to the study being described.

(e) This is a question about control of extraneous variables and you would need to say this for full marks. However, even someone who did not use the correct terminology might be able to offer a reasonable common-sense explanation. A word of advice here: in the research methods section there are often questions that can be answered reasonably correctly by using common-sense. Never leave a gap, even if you are not sure, as you could be lucky.

(f) Here your knowledge of ethical issues is tested. Several answers could be appropriate, although one particular issue stands out in the description of the study. Always try to use the BPS terminology when you refer to ethical issues. Note that this sub-section of the question is really in two parts, explanation and suggestion, and you must address both aspects to get full credit.

(g) **(i)** This is a straightforward question about unstructured interviews, although remember to elaborate sufficiently for 2 marks.

    (ii) You are asked to link what you know about unstructured interviews to the situation described in the text. Remember there is only 1 mark available here so you will only get 1 mark even if you offer more than one reason. If you do offer more than one, then the examiner will credit you for any one that is correct, but you will have wasted time that might have been better spent elsewhere.

question

(h) (i) You are simply asked to identify the sampling technique. If you know the correct term then a sentence is not necessary.

(ii) There is only 1 mark each for the strength and the limitation so you can make your answers quite brief.

■ ■ ■

Answer to question 5: candidate A

(a) Bar graph to show the mean response times for the two conditions.

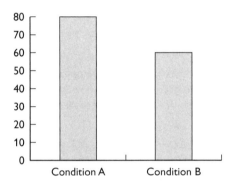

The graph is correctly plotted so scores 1 mark, but this candidate does not give a full title and the axis labels are incomplete/incorrect so no further marks are awarded.

(b) The mean is found by adding together all the scores and then dividing by the number of scores. It is a very sensitive measure of average. One problem is that the mean is quite difficult to calculate if there are a lot of scores.

This candidate starts by explaining how the mean is calculated, even though the question does not ask for that information. Many candidates waste time doing this and get no marks for it. In this case it is made worse as candidates give an advantage of using the mean, which is not asked for either. When he/she finally gets around to answering the question, he/she makes the mistake of giving a general point and not relating it to this study. In fact, we are not told how many partici- pants there are altogether so it may not be the case that 'there are lots of scores'. The correct answer here requires reference to the problem of using the mean where there are one or two very high or low scores. No marks for this part of the question.

(c) This is a repeated measures design with the same people in each condition.

1 mark is given here for correctly identifying the design.

(d) This is so that they don't all do better in the second condition because they have already had a go at the reaction time task and know what to expect.

📝 There is 1 mark here for noting the possibility of a practice effect (although this term is not used). There is no further explanation of the concept of order effects, nor is there any reference to the name of the technique (counterbalancing).

(e) This is so that the researcher can be sure that the times are not different because of the headphones rather than because of the type of stimulus.

📝 The candidate correctly explains the importance of controlling for extraneous variables, although neither the term 'control' nor the term 'extraneous variables' are used in the answer. This is a good example of a 1-mark common-sense answer.

(f) One ethical problem would be the upset caused to those participants who do not do very well. People should not be distressed or feel different about themselves because of what has happened in an experiment. This could have been avoided by sensitive handling.

📝 2 marks are awarded for an explanation of the issue although there is no use of BPS terminology. The candidate's attempt to address the second part of the question is a little vague and not worth a mark.

(g) (i) This is where there are no questions set beforehand and everyone has different questions.

📝 Although 2 marks are awarded here, it would have been a much better answer if there had been reference to how an unstructured interview starts with a general aim, or if the candidate had offered some expansion of the 'different questions' point.

(ii) It would be useful because you can find out things that the experiment maybe did not show: for example, if the person had a high reaction time for a reason.

📝 This suggestion is appropriate, relevant to the study in question and therefore worth a mark.

(h) (i) This is opportunity sampling.

📝 1 mark is awarded here.

(ii) One strength is that it is cheap. One limitation is that it would usually be applied to a limited range of people, so cannot be used to generalise the results.

📝 Candidates often refer to opportunity sampling as a 'cheap' method and it never gets any marks. The limitation is valid and is awarded 1 mark.

Total for this question: 11 out of 20 marks

Answer to question 5: candidate B

(a) Bar graph to show the mean response times in milliseconds in the light stimulus and noise stimulus conditions.

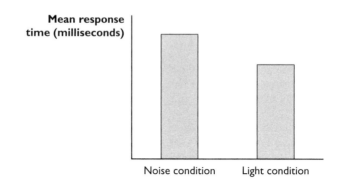

Mean response time (milliseconds)

Noise condition   Light condition

> The title gets a mark as it includes the units of measurement (milliseconds) and has the two named conditions (noise and light). The axis labels are correct for another mark. Although the plotting looks to be approximately correct, there are no units on the y-axis, which are required to get the third mark.

(b) In this study there is an extreme score (the person with the very high reaction time). This extreme score will distort the mean and make it higher than it really should be, making the mean less representative of the scores as a whole.

> 2 marks here for a correctly identified problem that relates directly to this study.

(c) Repeated measures design.

> 1 mark for identifying the experimental design.

(d) This is counterbalancing. It is necessary to control for the effects of order where participants perform in each condition. Performance in the second condition may be better because participants have had a practice, or it may be worse because they are tired (fatigue effect).

> This is a good 3-mark answer that includes a full explanation of the concept of order effects and names the technique correctly.

(e) This is to control for an extraneous variable and is to ensure that any difference in performance is not simply due to the wearing of headphones rather than the type of stimulus being responded to.

> This answer is awarded 2 marks for correctly identifying the issue using the appropriate terminology. Contrast this with the answer given by candidate A. Both candidates are aware of the key issue, but this answer shows evidence of study in the correct use of important methodological terminology.

(f) One ethical problem is protection from harm. The person who has a very high score in the light condition will be distressed by taking part in the study and so has not been protected from harm. This might have been avoided simply by not telling him outright that his score is much higher than everyone else's scores.

🖉 The key ethical issue in the study is identified using the BPS terminology for 1 mark. This is expanded for the second mark in a description of just how the person might be affected. The second half of the question is sensibly addressed for the third mark.

(g) (i) This is where there is a general aim in mind but no pre-determined questions. The researcher prompts the interviewee and can ask extra questions as issues arise.

🖉 This is a good 2-mark answer that includes reference to the aim instead of pre-set questions and the possibility of the questions being specific to the interviewee.

(ii) It might be useful to find out a reason why this person had a much higher score than other people, for example, perhaps he/she normally wears glasses but was not wearing glasses during the experiment.

🖉 1 mark is given for a sensible response linked directly to the study described in the question.

(h) (i) This is opportunity sampling.

🖉 1 mark is awarded.

(ii) This is a very quick method as you do not have to look out especially for people with particular characteristics. Bias is a problem though, because the researcher is choosing whoever he wants.

🖉 1 mark is awarded for the strength and 1 mark for the limitation. Notice there is evidence that the candidate understands both the issues. Had the candidate simply said that this method of sampling is 'quick' but possibly 'biased', the marks could not be awarded quite so confidently. Assertions like this should always be explained to be sure of credit.

Total for this question: 19 out of 20 marks

Research methods (II)

A team of psychologists set out to investigate the attitudes of university students towards healthy eating. They expect students on health-related courses to have a more positive attitude to healthy eating than students on other courses. They recruit a stratified sample of 200 university students from one university. They measure attitudes using a questionnaire about food preferences. The questionnaires are scored to give an overall 'preference for healthy food' score for each participant.

(a) Write a suitable hypothesis for this investigation.   (2 marks)

(b) Write an open question that could be used in the questionnaire.   (1 mark)

(c) Write a closed question that could be used in the questionnaire.   (1 mark)

(d) Identify *one* strength and *one* limitation of using open questions.   (2 marks)

(e) Explain how the psychologists might have selected a stratified sample of
　　students from the university.   (3 marks)

When the questionnaire data are analysed, the psychologists find that students are dissatisfied with the food at one of the university catering facilities. They decide to carry out a covert observation at this facility to observe students' behaviour. They are interested in whether students just eat there, or whether they use the facility for other purposes. They draw up a record chart for their observation.

(f) Explain what is meant by *covert observation* and suggest *one* reason why
　　psychologists might prefer to use a covert observation.   (2 marks)

(g) Draw a suitable record chart that the psychologists could use for their
　　observation showing at least *two* categories of behaviour.   (3 marks)

(h) Identify and explain *one* ethical issue involved in the observation.   (3 marks)

(i) In this case the psychologists carried out their observation in a natural
　　setting. Briefly discuss the use of natural observations.   (3 marks)

Total: 20 marks

(a) Here a full mark hypothesis should include conditions of both the independent variable and the dependent variable. These should be clearly stated and operationalised. Although the text points to a difference in a specific direction, at this level it does not matter whether you provide a directional hypothesis or simply predict a difference. A null hypothesis could also gain 2 marks here.

(b) This question must allow respondents to put any answer they like. Be careful not to use questions where the only sensible answer could be 'yes' or 'no'.

(c) The question should have a fixed number of optional answers, which you need to specify. Note that the questions for both (b) and (c) must be about food preferences to gain credit.

(d) Here the examiner is expecting a brief answer as you are simply asked to 'identify'. You do not need to use long sentences and could answer in note form to save time. You must, however, indicate clearly which is the strength and which is the limitation.

(e) This is worth 3 marks so you will need to offer some detail. Notice that this question is not asking you to define a stratified sample, but is asking how you would go about selecting a stratified sample from the population of students at one university.

(f) Here you get 1 mark for saying briefly what the term means, and the other mark for explaining why covert observations might be preferred.

(g) 1 mark is for the construction of some form of tally chart. The other 2 marks are for relevant categories of observable behaviours that might occur when the students use the catering facility.

(h) You are expected to identify a relevant ethical issue for the first mark. You should use the terminology from the BPS code of conduct here. The other 2 marks are for the explanation, which you should link to the study being considered here. In your explanation you could say why this particular ethical issue matters and why or how it should be taken into consideration.

(i) You will need to comment on the use of natural observations. There are various ways you could get the marks here. You could outline strengths and/or limitations of natural observations; or you could compare natural observations with the alternative, controlled observations.

■ ■ ■

Answer to question 6: candidate A

(a) Students on health courses have more positive attitudes to healthy food.

🖉 This is an incomplete hypothesis. It just about gets 1 mark because it is along the right lines.

(b) How often do you eat fresh vegetables in a week?

🖉 This is a valid example of an open question, relevant to the topic and worth 1 mark.

(c) Are you healthy? Yes/No

🖉 Although this is a closed question, it is not actually about food preferences so does not get the mark.

(d) Strength — any answer will do which is good. Limitation — people might not be able to think of anything to put down.

🖉 Neither the strength nor the limitation is good enough to be awarded a mark. No marks for this part of the question.

question

(e) A stratified sample means there are different groups like students from different courses. Some would be language students etc.

> 🖉 1 mark is awarded here because the candidate seems to have some understanding of the importance of sub-groups in a stratified sample.

(f) A covert observation is an undercover observation where no one can see the observer. This is better as people do not act up or show off in front of the observer.

> 🖉 Although not very well expressed, this is good enough for 2 marks.

(g) Record chart:

Chatting with friend	Alone reading	In large group

> 🖉 The record chart is suitable and has at least two valid categories so this section gets the full 3 marks.

(h) One ethical issue is asking consent. If you do not make the observer obvious, it means that people have not given their consent and cannot withdraw if they wish.

> 🖉 The issue of consent is a valid one and the candidate extends this a little by pointing out how one consequence of not gaining consent means that the participants cannot choose to withdraw from the study at any time. These two issues might be seen as separate ethical points, but they do overlap so 2 marks are gained here.

(i) A strength is that behaviour will be more normal and not artificial.

> 🖉 This is a 1-mark answer. For further marks the examiner would expect to see some elaboration, for example an explanation of how or why behaviour would be 'more normal'.

Total for this question: 11 out of 20 marks

■ ■ ■

Answer to question 6: candidate B

(a) Students on health-related courses will get a higher score on the questionnaire than students on non-health courses.

> 🖉 This is a good hypothesis with both conditions of the IV specified (types of course, i.e. health-related and non-health-related) and a clear DV (score on the questionnaire). 2 marks are awarded.

(b) Give the five types of food you most prefer.

> 🖉 This is a nice open question and worth 1 mark.

(c) Tick which of these you eat at least once a week:

Vegetables	Lean meat/fish	Beans/pulses	Whole cereals

📝 This is a good closed question and gets **1 mark**.

(d) One strength is that the responses are more likely to be valid as people can be quite truthful and say their real answer. The problem is in analysis as there are no categories so it is difficult to see patterns and do graphs.

📝 Both the strength and the limitation are valid so each gets **1 mark**.

(e) They would need participants from different groups in the population. They could divide up the students according to year or type of course. Then they need to select from each group in ratio according to how many there are for each group in the population. So, if there are more students in Year 1, then there should be more in the sample from Year 1. The final selection should be randomly done.

📝 This is a full 3-mark answer. The candidate has correctly noted the key issues involved in stratified sampling: identification of sub-groups, representation in proportion, random selection from each sub-group.

(f) This is where the observer cannot be seen by those being observed. This helps to ensure that the behaviour being observed is more natural.

📝 Both elements are here so this answer gets **2 marks**.

(g) Record chart to record frequencies of observed behaviours.

	Eating	Reading
Frequency tally		

📝 The record chart is suitable and has two valid categories. This answer gets **3 marks**.

(h) A key issue is informed consent. Ideally participants should give consent and know what they are consenting to. However, in this study it would make the observation pointless. The BPS code states that privacy should not be infringed and that observations are alright if carried out in a public place, such as the canteen, because people would normally expect to be observed there. In this case there is no need to ask for consent because they are in a public place.

📝 The issues of consent and privacy are both relevant and each of these alone could have formed the basis of an answer. Here they are rather cleverly linked so all the content is deemed relevant and the answer is therefore fully elaborated to get the full 3 marks.

question

(i) This means that the results have greater validity. The behaviour is more true to life because the study takes place in a real-life context. In controlled observations you are less likely to see true behaviours because they are occurring out of their usual context.

   This answer gets 3 marks. Although the issue is the same as that expressed by the previous candidate, this answer is rather more impressive because the candidate uses the correct terminology, referring to 'context' and 'validity'. He/she has followed the instruction to discuss by presenting some comparison with the alternative type of observation.

Total for this question: 20 out of 20 marks